Pullin' the Wool

A comedy

Frank Vickery

Samuel French — London
New York - Toronto - Hollywood

© 2002 BY FRANK VICKERY

Rights of Performance by Amateurs are controlled by Samuel French Ltd, 52 Fitzroy Street, London W1T 5JR, and they, or their authorized agents, issue licences to amateurs on payment of a fee. **It is an infringement of the Copyright to give any performance or public reading of the play before the fee has been paid and the licence issued.**

The Royalty Fee indicated below is subject to contract and subject to variation at the sole discretion of Samuel French Ltd.

> Basic fee for each and every
> performance by amateurs   Code M
> in the British Isles

The Professional Repertory Rights in this plays are controlled by Samuel French Ltd. Professional Rights, other than Repertory Rights, are controlled by Bill McLean Personal Management, 23b Deodar Road, Putney, London SW15 2NP

The publication of this play does not imply that it is necessarily available for performance by amateurs or professionals, either in the British Isles or Overseas. Amateurs and professionals considering a production are strongly advised in their own interests to apply to the appropriate agents for written consent before starting rehearsals or booking a theatre or hall.

ISBN 0 573 01959 2

Please see page iv for further copyright information

PULLIN' THE WOOL

First produced by the Sherman Theatre Company at The Sherman Theatre, Cardiff, on 6th October, 1998, with the following cast:

Ray Gibbon	Rhys Miles Thomas
Sheila Gibbon	Shelley Rees
Martyn Walsh	Phylip Harries
Gayle Walsh	Kathryn Dimery
Barrie Lovejoy/Dave	David Middleton
Denise Lovejoy/Di	Helen Griffin

Directed by **Phil Clark**
Lighting design by **Chris Barrett**

COPYRIGHT INFORMATION

(See also page ii)

This play is fully protected under the Copyright Laws of the British Commonwealth of Nations, the United States of America and all countries of the Berne and Universal Copyright Conventions.

All rights including Stage, Motion Picture, Radio, Television, Public Reading, and Translation into Foreign Languages, are strictly reserved.

No part of this publication may lawfully be reproduced in ANY form or by any means—photocopying, typescript, recording (including video-recording), manuscript, electronic, mechanical, or otherwise—or be transmitted or stored in a retrieval system, without prior permission.

Licences for amateur performances are issued subject to the understanding that it shall be made clear in all advertising matter that the audience will witness an amateur performance; that the names of the authors of the plays shall be included on all programmes; and that the integrity of the authors' work will be preserved.

The Royalty Fee is subject to contract and subject to variation at the sole discretion of Samuel French Ltd.

In Theatres or Halls seating Four Hundred or more the fee will be subject to negotiation.

In Territories Overseas the fee quoted above may not apply. A fee will be quoted on application to our local authorized agent, or if there is no such agent, on application to Samuel French Ltd, London.

VIDEO-RECORDING OF AMATEUR PRODUCTIONS

Please note that the copyright laws governing video-recording are extremely complex and that it should not be assumed that any play may be video-recorded for whatever purpose without first obtaining the permission of the appropriate agents. The fact that a play is published by Samuel French Ltd does not indicate that video rights are available or that Samuel French Ltd controls such rights.

CHARACTERS

Ray Gibbon
Sheila Gibbon
Martyn Walsh
Gayle Walsh
Barrie Lovejoy
Denise Lovejoy
Dave
Di

The action of the play takes place simultaneously in the living-rooms of the Walshes and the Gibbons on a Friday and Saturday evening a week apart in the middle of June.

ACT I   Before the meal

ACT II   After the drinks

Time: the present

**Other plays by Frank Vickery
published by Samuel French Ltd**

Full Length
All's Fair
Biting the Bullet
Breaking the String
Easy Terms
Erogenous Zones
Family Planning
A Kiss on the Bottom
Loose Ends
Love Forty
A Night on the Tiles
One O'Clock From the House
Spanish Lies
Roots and Wings
Trivial Pursuits

One-act
After I'm Gone
Green Favours
A Night Out
Split Ends

ACT I

The set is the living-room of the Walsh family and the living-room of the Gibbon family. The Walsh element is newish and tasteful, the Gibbon half is older and thoughtless in terms of its decor. There should be a sharp and obvious contrast between the two

At the back R on the Walsh side, there is a door which leads to the hall and upstairs. Near the back is a stand on which there is a stereo unit. In the Gibbon half L is a door which leads to the same layout. In-between these and along the back wall are two halves of a dresser. One perhaps more of a display kind of cabinet on the Walsh side and a battered old-fashioned type of sideboard for the Gibbons. In the middle of the room C is a large rug. One half has a Chinese look, the other is a badly stained nylon off-cut type of carpet. Either side and angled towards the fourth wall are two sofas, one very modern and the other looking in a very distressed state. Upstage of the Walshes' sofa is a small low table with a phone on it. Similarly, there is a cheap and cheerful looking table DL of the Gibbons' sofa, again with a phone on it. A door UR leads to the Walshes' dining-room, DR is the door to their kitchen. On the wall opposite and in the Gibbons' half is the kitchen door DL. Upstage and further along the wall is a drinks bar, the sort that was never fashionable but came into existence about the mid to late Sixties. A large coffee table is DC, half in each room. The Walshes' half has a lace cloth and table centre on it, the Gibbons' half is bare wood with a fruit bowl filled with junk

When the CURTAIN *rises no-one is on stage*

After a short while, Ray comes in barefoot from the hall

He makes for the settee and reaches for an enormous spliff he rolled earlier. He lights it before starting to cut his toe nails with rather large scissors. Having cut one, he carefully places it on the coffee table, presumably along with several others

There is a noise, off, as Sheila trips over a pair of ladders out in the hall and screams from just outside the room

Sheila (*off*) Jesus Christ, Ray! 'Ow many times 'ave I got to tell you to shift those bloody ladders.

Sheila comes in, limping and carrying two light raincoats, one for Ray and one for herself

Ray I'll do it tomorrow. (*He drags on his spliff*)
Sheila Ay, I've 'eard ducks fart before. (*She sniffs*) Are you on tha' wacky backy again?
Ray Want one?
Sheila Bugger off. I thought you said you were ready.
Ray I am, just 'bout.
Sheila Do you *'ave* to cut your toe nails in 'ere?
Ray Does it matter where I cut 'em, as long as I put 'em in the bin after?
Sheila But you don't, though, do you? I've found one in my omelette before now.
Ray Tha's why I don't cut 'em in the kitchen any more.

There is a roll of thunder

Sheila (*putting Ray's coat on the back of the sofa and putting her own on*) You'd better wear this, Ray, it's pissin' down out there. We'll be like a pair of drowned rats now by the time we get to the Walshes'.
Ray We're not goin' to get wet in the car, mun.
Sheila God knows where you're goin' to park it. There's double yellow lines everywhere, if you remember.
Ray Up 'is drive, innit? There's room for two.
Sheila (*smiling at the thought*) Imagine when we move, Ray ... us with a drive tha' big. Per'aps we can afford tha' little runaround you promised me, then.
Ray I wouldn't put your mind on it. Everythin' depends on wha' we get their 'ouse for.
Sheila You were sortin' tha' out, you said.
Ray I am. I've got a plan. Now all I got to do is carry it out ... tonight.
Sheila (*not affectionately*) I've got every confidence in you, sweet'eart.
Ray At the end of the day it's not up to me, though, is it? Everythin' 'angs on whether they take the bait or not.

A beat as Sheila puts on her lipstick, looking in the mirror in the fourth wall

Sheila 'Ave you phoned 'em? The Walshes.
Ray No.
Sheila I said we would.
Ray We don't 'ave to.
Sheila But I've said.
Ray There's no need, mun.

Act I

Sheila But I've *said* now.
Ray Well, phone 'em, then.
Sheila You, I've got to go to the bathroom.

Sheila rushes out of the room

Ray You got the trots or wha'? (*He starts putting on his socks*)
Sheila (*shouting, leaving*) Just phone 'em!

Sheila exits

Another roll of thunder. Ray, who has now put on his socks, goes to the phone and dials. The phone in Martyn's house rings. It rings several times before Gayle is heard calling from the kitchen

Gayle (*off; calling, a little impatiently*) Martyn, can you get that?

There is no reply

Martyn?

Again no reply

Gayle comes out of the kitchen with both arms bent at the elbow, her hands are covered in white powder. She is wearing a rather nice dress with an apron over it

With the phone still ringing, she calls into the hallway

Martyn, I'm up to my wrists in breadcrumbs down here, can you take it upstairs?

At this point Ray hangs up. The phone stops ringing

Thank you. (*She appears to be satisfied that Martyn has answered it*)

Gayle returns to the kitchen

Ray decides to have a drink, a vodka or gin or anything that comes to hand that's on the bar. After pouring, he is about to drink, when he spots something floating in the glass. He takes it out and shakes it between his thumb and finger before looking at it. Recognising it, he tuts and places it on the coffee table along with the rest of his toe nails

Sheila (*off; calling from the hallway*) Ray, 'ave you seen my umbrella?
Ray I thought you 'ad to go to the bathroom.
Sheila (*off; insisting*) 'Ave you?
Ray No.
Sheila (*off*) Are you sure? It was 'angin' on the back of the door this mornin'.
Ray 'Ave a look on the back of the door, then.
Sheila (*off*) Oh, very bloody funny.

Ray sighs and casually goes out to the hallway to help her look for it. Taking his drink with him, he calls to her as he goes

Ray I thought I saw it up in the bath last.

As Ray leaves the room, Martyn enters from his hallway. He is almost dressed and has a wooden ball from the base of the stair-rail in his hand

Taking a cigarette out of his mouth, Martyn speaks

Martyn Gayle, you wouldn't believe what's just come off in my ... hand. (*Realizing Gayle isn't in the room. He calls*) Gayle?
Gayle (*from the kitchen off*) In here.
Martyn (*spotting his tie on the back of the sofa*) Oh, Gayle ... do I really have to wear a tie tonight?
Gayle (*off*) Absolutely.
Martyn It's only the Gibbons for God's sake. (*He puts the cigarette back in his mouth*)

Gayle enters

Gayle I don't care. If we don't make an effort, Martyn, heaven knows they won't. (*She takes the cigarette out of Martyn's mouth and stubs it in an ashtray*) You can't smoke in here, I've sprayed.
Martyn You had a cigarette earlier on.
Gayle That was my last until tomorrow. I don't want this place smelling like we're smokers.
Martyn But we are smokers.
Gayle That's not the point. (*A beat as she notices the wooden ball in his hand. She sighs as she looks around the room*) My God, what's that?
Martyn I didn't know it was loose; did you?
Gayle Can you put it back?
Martyn (*nodding*) Yes ... if I've got time.
Gayle Make time. (*She takes it from him*) Trust it to come off tonight. Between what happened to the bathroom cabinet yesterday, and the stair

Act I

carpet the day before, I'm beginning to wonder if there aren't some ... forces at work.

There is a rumble of thunder from not too far away

Martyn Now you're being silly.
Gayle The place is falling apart, Martyn.

Martyn takes the wooden ball back from her and places it on the dresser

Martyn No, it's not, what's wrong is just cosmetic. The structure is as sound as a bell, I love this house.
Gayle (*checking her appearance in the mirror in the fourth wall*) God knows what the Gibbons will do when they get their hands on it. I bet a year from now we won't recognize the place. Who was on the phone?
Martyn When?
Gayle Just now.
Martyn I don't know.
Gayle You answered it.
Martyn No.
Gayle I called you. "I'm busy, answer the phone", I said.
Martyn Sorry, didn't hear it ... or *you* either. (*He is putting on the tie as he spots Gayle's dress*) Is that new?
Gayle What?
Martyn Under the apron.
Gayle The dress? Good heavens, no... I've had this in the wardrobe for months. (*She hasn't. She is eager to change the subject*) Look at the state of the place, what a *mess*.

It's perfection. She proceeds to puff cushions and rearrange a few things

Martyn You're not serious?
Gayle I can't have people seeing it like this, Martyn. Have I got time to get the Hoover out?
Martyn You only put it away ten minutes ago.
Gayle When selling a house it's important the prospective purchasers see it at its best. There should always be something cooking in the kitchen. (*She gestures towards the kitchen door*) And plenty of lamps on in the lounge. (*She switches each of the two lamps on*)
Martyn Gayle, they've already seen it. They're buying it, for God's sake.
Gayle Nothing has been signed.
Martyn Yes, I know that, but——
Gayle Don't argue with me—get the Hoover out.

Martyn It's fine, Gayle.

Another roll of thunder

Everything's fine. You can practically see your face in the carpet as it is.
Gayle (*after a slight pause*) Well, if you're sure.
Martyn I'm positive. The aroma's wonderful and the lights are flattering.

Another clap of thunder... nearer this time

(*Sitting on the sofa*) I just hope the weather isn't going to put them off. Still, they've got a car ... if you can call it a car.
Gayle Perhaps it's an antique. What make is it?
Martyn A Hillman Imp.
Gayle Never heard of it ... probably worth a fortune.
Martyn If that car is worth anything to anyone, Gayle, it's to a scrap merchant. They didn't look as if they could afford to *tax* the thing, let alone buy a place like this.
Gayle You can't always see money, though, Martyn, can you?
Martyn No ... and they do have a house to sell.
Gayle That is amazing. I had them down for a council flat and a life on social security.
Martyn (*sighing*) Still, they've got a mortgage.
Gayle (*suspiciously*) Yes.
Martyn The surveyor came weeks ago ... we would have heard from them if they'd been refused.

Gayle still looks a little doubtful. Martyn thinks about this for a brief moment, then convinces himself

They're coming to dinner, for God's sake ... they'd hardly accept our invitation if things weren't going ahead.
Gayle It wasn't a proper invitation. If you remember, Martyn, they more or less invited themselves.
Martyn I don't think so.
Gayle Martyn, they pulled a fast one ... the last time they viewed, we gave them coffee ... *he* said something about how they don't get out much, *she* complimented me on my Tiramisu and the next thing all this was arranged.
Martyn (*smiling as he catches her around the waist*) *I* think it's great they're coming tonight.
Gayle *You're* not doing the cooking.
Martyn Having them round for a meal is just what we need.
Gayle What for?

Act I

Martyn The smell ... the ambience...
Gayle (*suspiciously*) What are you up to?

Another roll of thunder

Martyn (*playfully*) You're just going to have to wait and see, aren't you?

In the Gibbons' part, Sheila comes in from the hall, followed by Ray

Sheila heads for the kitchen

Sheila If it's not in the kitchen I don't know where it is.
Ray We'll go as we are. A drop of rain won't 'arm us.
Martyn (*to Gayle*) How are things in the kitchen?
Gayle All right. I'm sure someone told me you could grill spinach.
Sheila I'm not goin' nowhere without somethin' on my 'ead. Can't go to the Walshes' with my 'air all bloody limp and 'orrible, can I?

Ray doesn't answer, he just looks at her, at her hair

Gayle I haven't given up on it yet. Improvise, that's what Delia says.

Martyn tries to steal a kiss

Careful, Martyn! I spent all afternoon in the hairdressers.
Sheila I bet tha' *Gayle* 'ave spent all afternoon in the 'airdressers.
Martyn You should have bought a Savoy.
Gayle And give them *cabbage*?
Sheila I'm not 'avin' 'er think she's any better than me. (*She sits and quickly slips her shoes on*) Did you phone 'em like I said?
Ray Ay. (*He begins to look for something*)
Gayle The recipe says *spinach*, Martyn.
Martyn So, what culinary delights are you thrilling us with?
Sheila Wha'd they say?
Ray They didn't say nothin'.
Gayle We're having a warm duck salad to start.
Ray I couldn't get an answer.
Sheila Well, try again, then.

Sheila goes off into the kitchen

Gayle And the main course is *épinards à la niçoise*.
Martyn Cabbage would have been fine.

Ray I don't think they're there. (*He begins to look for something*)
Sheila (*off*) They've asked us round for a bit of grub, they've got to bloody be there.
Gayle It hardly has the same ring to it, does it? "Riviera cabbage?"
Ray Where's tha' brown envelope gone now?
Martyn It's better they enjoy the food than its name.
Gayle Oh, they won't enjoy the meal, Martyn. It's far too sophisticated for their taste.
Ray It was by 'ere five minutes ago.
Martyn What did you cook it for, then?
Gayle I like saying it.
Sheila (*off*) Wha's it look like?
Ray Wha'd you mean, wha's it look like? It's brown ... and it looks like a bloody envelope.
Gayle (*savouring it*) "Épinards à la niçoise".
Ray Are you sure you 'aven't put it anywhere?
Sheila (*off; shouting*) I 'aven't bloody seen it.
Gayle Now you make sure you ask me at least twice in front of them what we're eating tonight.
Ray Sheila, you're goin' to 'ave to come in and 'elp me.
Sheila (*off*) Ray, I'm lookin' for my umbrella.
Martyn That's right, you soften them up with some posh nosh.
Gayle Why? We're not going to get a penny more out of them.
Ray (*still looking*) Well, *I* don't know where the 'ell it's gone.
Martyn We can try. At the end of the day we've got to look after number one, Gayle. By the time we add on a couple of hundred for this, and a couple of hundred for that...
Sheila (*off*) It's all right, I've found it.
Ray The envelope?
Sheila The brolly.
Martyn We could bump the price up by a thousand or two.
Gayle They'll never go for it.

Sheila comes in from the kitchen with the brolly

Sheila Right, well, I'm ready when you are.
Martyn They might. They're desperate to buy this house.
Ray We're not goin' anywhere till we find tha' envelope.
Martyn *Absolutely* desperate.
Sheila Why, wha's in it?
Ray You don't want to know.
Martyn You don't know what lengths they'd go to secure the place.
Sheila Tell me wha' you're up to.

Act I

Gayle They're not stupid, Martyn ... they'll smell a rat.
Martyn (*sniffing*) *I* can smell something too.
Gayle Oh God!

Realizing something is burning in the kitchen, Gayle rushes out in a panic

Martyn Èpinards a la knackered by the whiff of it. (*He pours himself a drink*)
Sheila Come on, Ray, I'm waitin'.
Ray It's the surveyor's report in it. I've 'ad a fake one drawn up.
Sheila (*excitedly*) You 'aven't! Who done tha' for you?
Ray One of my contacts, innit. (*Smiling broadly*) You should see it, Sheil', it pulls their place to pieces.
Sheila Wha' if they suspect somethin'?
Ray They won't, it's a work of art. Now all you've got to do is leave everything to me, and with a bit of luck and the wind behind us, we'll 'ave tha' 'ouse for the price we want.
Sheila Providin' you find tha' envelope.
Ray It's a mystery to me. Go 'n' 'ave a look upstairs, will you, love?
Sheila (*going*) You're always the bloody same, you are. Ring the Walshes again.

Sheila goes off up to the bedroom

Ray helps himself to another drink first. Another roll of thunder... but from a distance. The door chimes go in the Walshes'

Gayle comes to stand in the kitchen doorway, almost rigid with fear

Gayle Is that the front door?
Martyn (*making a little joke*) Unless it's the smoke alarm.

Door chimes go again

Gayle It is, it's the front door. My God, Martyn, it's them, they're here.
Martyn (*checking his watch*) They're half an hour early.
Gayle (*panicking*) I'm not ready for them.
Martyn What do you want me to do?
Gayle Tell them to come back in half an hour.
Martyn I can't do that.
Gayle Explain, they'll understand.
Martyn Gayle, it's like a monsoon out there.

The bell chimes a third time

Gayle (*screaming*) I don't believe this! How could they do this to me? I haven't even balled the melon.

Almost in tears, Gayle turns and goes back into the kitchen

Martyn goes off to answer the front door

Ray picks up the phone and dials. The phone rings in the Walshes'

Martyn (*off*) Oh, hallo. This is a surprise.

Denise enters

Denise Took a gamble. Thought we'd call in on the off chance. Parked up your drive.

Martyn and Barrie follow Denise in

Barrie Hope that's all right?

The phone is still ringing

Martyn Excuse me a minute. (*He answers the phone*) Hallo?
Ray Hallo?
Martyn (*after a slight pause*) Who is this?
Ray You are there, then?
Martyn Sorry?
Ray It's Ray... Ray Gibbon.
Martyn Oh, hallo... Mr Gibbon. Ray. Everything all right?
Ray Fine, ay, as far as I know.
Martyn Good. (*He pauses slightly*) You're still coming round?
Ray Yes, ay.
Martyn I thought for a minute you were ringing to cancel.
Ray No.
Martyn So you were ringing about something else, were you?
Ray No.
Martyn Oh.
Ray Sheila said to give you a call, tha's all.
Martyn I see.
Ray (*after a slight pause*) So I'm just givin' you a call.
Martyn (*after a slight pause; almost suspiciously*) Right.
Ray Right. (*He pauses slightly*) We'll see you in a bit, then.
Martyn Yes. (*He pauses slightly*) Bye.

Act I

Both Martyn and Ray hang up, but Ray doesn't replace his receiver properly. Martyn looks over at Barrie and smiles rather awkwardly

Martyn (*Explaining*) Mr Gibbon. The next one down in the chain.
Ray (*calling to Sheila*) I've rung 'em. (*He sits and puts on his shoes*)
Denise Bad time, is it?
Martyn Sorry?
Denise To call.
Martyn No.
Denise Barrie said to ring.
Barrie I did, yes.
Denise We can call again.
Martyn No, not at all.
Denise Only we just thought, you know...
Barrie On the off chance.
Martyn It's all right.
Barrie (*to Denise*) I said to ring first.
Martyn Let me take your coat.
Barrie We won't stay long. (*He produces a bottle of wine from behind and hands it to Martyn*)
Denise (*taking off her coat*) Feel really awful about this.
Martyn No, don't...

Barrie starts to take off his coat

Denise (*to Barrie*) See? Told you t'would be all right. (*To Martyn*) I said you wouldn't mind.
Barrie (*handing his coat to Martyn*) One drink and we're off.

Denise hands Martyn her coat too

Martyn (*after a slight pause; to Gayle in the kitchen*) Gayle?
Gayle (*off*) Yes?
Martyn Come and see who's here.

Barrie and Denise stand positioned with the broadest of smiles

Gayle enters from the kitchen

Gayle Hallo, hallo, every... (*She stops in her tracks when she sees them*) Mr and Mrs Lovejoy. (*Her face twitches*)
Denise Oh, Barrie and Denise, please.
Martyn They just popped in.

Denise On the off chance. We could have had a solicitor drop a line——
Barrie But I said no.
Denise These things are best settled over a bottle of wine.
Gayle There's nothing wrong, is there?
Martyn You're still selling us your house?
Denise (*enthusiastically*) Of course.
Barrie (*very positive*) Oh, yes. Absolutely.
Denise Absolutely. (*Beat*) It's just that we've decided to take a few bits and bobs with us, you know.
Martyn I see.
Gayle Such as?
Barrie We can discuss all that later.
Denise In the meantime, hope you can lay your hands on a decent corkscrew? (*She takes the bottle of wine from Barrie and holds it up. She smells the air*) Oooh, something smells appetising.
Gayle (*flattered and gloating*) It's only something I've quickly thrown together. (*She nods at Martyn in an attempt at prompting him to ask what she is cooking*)

Martyn doesn't click on immediately; when he does, he plays his part, but very unnaturally

Martyn What are we having, sweetheart?
Gayle Épinards à la niçoise.
Denise (*realizing*) You're about to eat. We shouldn't have come. (*She takes their coats from Martyn*)
Gayle (*oozing with charm and possibly over-doing it*) Nonsense. You must join us.
Martyn The more the merrier.
Gayle There's plenty to go round.

Denise hands Barrie his coat

You must, I insist.
Denise It's out of the question.
Martyn (*making a joke of it*) Gayle will take it personally if you don't.
Gayle I would.
Denise You would? (*She looks at Gayle*)

Gayle is reluctant to agree but nods as she can't do anything else in the circumstances

Gayle I would.

Act I

Denise Well ... when you put it like that.
Gayle It's settled, then.

Denise takes back Barrie's coat and hands it once again to Martyn, along with her own

Denise Well, if we're staying to dinner—Barrie, keys?

Barrie drops them into the palm of her open hand

   I just need to make a phone call on the car phone.

   Denise leaves

There is a slight pause

Martyn Well, then, Barrie, take a seat.
Barrie Er, I wonder if I might use the bathroom.
Gayle Yes, of course. Top of the stairs, first left.
Martyn Come on, I'll show you.
Gayle (*smiling but with an edge of condescension*) I'm sure Barrie can find it on his own, Martyn. (*To Barrie*) Our bedroom door is ajar so you might catch a glimpse of the fitted bedroom we put in last year.
Martyn We're leaving that for the Gibbons now of course ... a gift. We wouldn't think of charging them for it.

Gayle forcefully shows Barrie out of the room

Barrie (*off*) First door on the left, you said?
Gayle (*almost singing it*) Yes, that's right. You can't miss it, it's the door just past the rather nice jardinière.
Martyn (*chirpily*) We're leaving that as well. (*He laughs*)

Gayle laughs too as she closes the door firmly behind them. Her laughter immediately turns to tears

   In the Gibbons' half, Sheila comes in from upstairs

   (*To Gayle*) Why are you upset?
Sheila (*to Ray*) It's not upstairs.
Gayle It's going to be a nightmare.
Ray Are you sure?
Sheila You bloody look, then.

Gayle (*grasping for an idea*) You're going to have to phone the Gibbons.
Sheila (*insisting*) Go on.
Gayle And put them off.
Martyn I can't do that.
Ray Well, it's a mystery to me.
Gayle (*her nerves are raw*) They couldn't possibly come now.
Sheila I wish you'd stop sayin' "it's a mystery to me".
Gayle They just can't.
Sheila And get up off your bloody arse.
Gayle (*trying not to cry*) Not now—not tonight.
Ray (*getting up*) I 'ad it in my 'and five minutes ago.
Martyn It's only a meal, for heaven's sake.
Gayle For *four*.
Sheila *You* 'ave a look upstairs.
Gayle I'm cooking for *four*.
Martyn Portion it out.
Gayle (*almost hysterical*) It's Nouvelle Cuisine. Jesus Christ couldn't stretch it any further.
Sheila Go on, Ray ... or we'll never bloody get there.
Martyn Well, why did you invite them?
Gayle I panicked.

Ray reluctantly goes off upstairs

I panicked and said the first thing that came into my head.
Sheila (*calling after Ray*) I'll 'ave another look down 'ere.
Gayle Why couldn't you have kept them on the door ... told them we had guests coming?
Martyn They were standing in the hall two seconds after taking off the chain-lock.

During the following, Sheila looks for the brown envelope

Gayle I don't like it, Martyn.
Martyn What?
Gayle Them turning up like this. I mean, they're practically strangers and they turn up here without so much as a phone call... (*She has a thought*) They didn't phone, did they?
Martyn No.
Gayle (*scornfully*) Martyn.
Martyn No, definitely not, no.

Gayle looks suspiciously at him

Act I

Well, you heard them. They called in on the off chance.
Gayle *And* it's raining.
Martyn Sorry?
Gayle We've only met them twice. Two viewings and they arrive, uninvited, in the pouring rain with a bottle of wine and a smile ... it's not something you do ... unless you have an ulterior motive, which believe me if they have, Martyn, is bad news.
Martyn (*trying to reassure her*) It's not that bad.
Gayle You know what it is?
Martyn Well, it's obvious. They've got their little list of what they're leaving and what they're not. They've come to squeeze some money out of us.
Gayle (*outraged*) That's disgusting.
Martyn I know. Don't you just hate people who take advantage? (*He winks*)

Sheila finds the envelope on the bar

Sheila (*calling to Ray upstairs*) I got it!
Gayle What happens now?
Martyn Well, we can't afford to upset them. Rub them up the wrong way and they might not leave us so much as a light bulb.
Gayle Offend the Gibbons and they could withdraw their offer.

Ray comes back in from upstairs

He looks over at Sheila who is sitting down waving the envelope in the air

Ray Where'd you find tha'?
Sheila It was only right in front of your bloody eyes, wan' it.
Gayle I'm sorry, Martyn, there's no way I could possibly cope with the Lovejoys *and* the Gibbons here tonight.
Ray Come on, then, girl ... let's get goin'.

Ray takes the envelope from Sheila as he reaches for a pack of lager from the top of the trolley

Gayle You're definitely going to have to put them off.
Martyn But I've just spoken to him. What will I say?
Sheila Where you think you're goin' with tha'?
Gayle Say anything. Improvise.
Ray It's only a couple a lagers.
Sheila We're not takin' *lagers* with us.
Gayle Tell them I've been rushed to hospital with a nervous breakdown. No, that's silly.

Sheila You want 'em to think we're bloody common or somethin'? When people ask you for a meal, Ray, you take a nice bottle of wine.
Ray We 'aven't got wine.
Gayle (*attempting to pull herself together*) Do you think I could have a cigarette? I need one.

Martyn takes two cigarettes out of the packet and lights them both

Sheila (*taking a bottle from under the trolley*) It's lucky I thought to buy this this mornin', then, innit?
Gayle (*thinking aloud*) It's all right ... everything will be all right as long as we put the Gibbons off.

Martyn hands a cigarette to Gayle

Ray What wine is it?
Gayle Try and think of something.
Sheila I don't know.
Martyn Perhaps we could say we're down with food poisoning.
Gayle (*outraged*) Don't you dare!

Martyn puts the lighter down on the coffee table

Sheila I don't know nothin' about wine, do I?
Gayle She might think it's my cooking. (*Improvising*) Tell them you're having a heart attack and I'm driving you to the hospital.
Sheila 'Ave you locked everythin' up now?
Martyn If I'm having a heart attack, shouldn't *you* be ringing them? (*He takes a drag on his cigarette*)
Ray Yes.
Gayle Absolutely not. I've got far more important things to do in the kitchen. (*She snatches the cigarette from Martyn's mouth and stubs it out*)

  Gayle goes into the kitchen

Sheila The back door?
Ray Yes.

Martyn sighs and reluctantly phones the Gibbons

Sheila The windows?
Ray Ay.
Sheila Switched the timer on the lamp?

Act I   17

Ray (*looking at his watch*) Should be comin' on any second now.

Ray looks from his watch to the lamp at the same time as Sheila does

Martyn (*calling to Gayle*) It's engaged.
Gayle (*off*) Try again.

Suddenly, the table lamp in the Gibbon area comes on. Ray smiles back at Sheila

Martyn dials again, but gets the engaged signal

Martyn (*calling off*) Can't we let them come and be damned with it?
Gayle (*off; absolutely determined*) Just keep ringing!

Martyn dials immediately

Sheila Well, tha's it, then, is it?

Ray nods. Taking one last look around the room, Sheila spots the phone hasn't been replaced properly

   Look, you've done it again, 'aven't you?

Again Martyn gets the engaged signal and puts the phone down impatiently

   You never put the bloody phone back tidy, you don't. (*She replaces the receiver*)
Ray (*picking up his coat from the back of the sofa*) Well, I can't do everythin'!

As they are about to leave the room, Sheila fiddles with her umbrella and in the process pushes it inside out

Sheila Oh, look at tha' now.
Ray (*snatching it from her*) Give it 'ere.

   Ray and Sheila go off into the hallway

Gayle (*off*) Any luck?

Martyn quickly picks up the receiver again and dials

Sheila (*off*) Oh, there's nice ... goin' to fix it for me, are you?

Ray (*off*) No, I'm goin' to throw it in the bloody bin!

There's a crash. Ray screams

(*Off*) Tha' fuckin' ladder!

We hear Sheila laugh hysterically before she slams the front door closed

A few seconds after they have left, their phone rings

Martyn (*calling to Gayle*) Gayle, it's ringing.

Gayle comes in from the kitchen, looking very uptight and still with a cigarette

Gayle Don't forget, you're in a terrible state and waiting for the ambulance.
Martyn I thought you were driving me?
Gayle (*confused, but remembering*) Oh, yes. Well, in any case, you're in a bad way.
Martyn If I'm that ill, it's definitely *you* who should be on the phone.
Gayle (*after a slight pause; giving in reluctantly*) Oh, give it to me, for goodness sake. (*She takes the receiver and listens, and waits, and waits. On the verge of tears*) They're not there. (*She still waits and listens*) I can't believe it. (*She breaks down*) They must be on their way. What am I going to do?

All the Lights fade in the Gibbons house

Martyn goes over to Gayle, takes the receiver and hangs it up, takes the cigarette from her hand as he puts his arm around her in an attempt to comfort her

Martyn It'll be all right. (*He takes a quick drag*) There must be *something* we can give them to eat?

Gayle cries even more

Barrie and Denise come in from upstairs

Martyn and Gayle scramble to make things look normal. Gayle waves her hands in the air, trying to get rid of the smoke

Denise Hope it's not bad news or anything?

Act I

Gayle (*frantically trying to pull herself together*) No, no, it's fine.
Martyn She's fine.
Denise Are you sure?
Martyn Yes, it happens all the time.
Denise (*very interested*) Really? (*To Martyn*) How often would you say? Two or three times a week?

Martyn looks very uncomfortable and shrugs

   A day perhaps?

No-one answers. After a moment or two, Martyn, improvising madly, offers an answer

Martyn Every time we eat them.
Denise (*ignoring Martyn's answer as she zooms in on Gayle*) Want to talk to me about it, dear?
Gayle About what?
Denise (*to Martyn and Barrie*) Denial, that's typical. (*To Gayle*) Sometimes it helps to talk to another woman.
Gayle Sorry?
Martyn (*still trying to rescue the situation*) I did offer to peel them.
Denise (*taking Gayle and sitting her down on the sofa*) Men never understand what we go through.
Gayle I don't know what you're on about.
Denise (*sitting next to her*) I'm exactly the same myself.
Martyn Onions.

No-one really takes notice of him

Denise One minute I'm quite normal and the next—weeping buckets.
Martyn Onions, yes. That's all it is. Tell her, Gayle.

Gayle looks at Denise who in turn looks at Martyn

Denise With all due respect, Martyn ... it's all right for me to call you Martyn, is it?
Martyn Of course.
Denise With all due respect, it's obvious to me that, Gayle ... is it all right?
Gayle For you to call me Gayle, yes.
Denise Well, in my opinion, Gayle, what's wrong with you has nothing at all to do with onions.
Gayle I agree.

Denise You're completely stressed out.
Gayle I am?
Martyn No, she's not.
Gayle (*standing*) Yes, I am.
Denise Saw it immediately.
Martyn (*raising his voice*) Tell them it's the onions, Gayle. (*He makes a face at her as he points frantically to both eyes*)
Gayle (*confused, beginning to cry again*) Yes, it's the onions.
Denise Sorry, Martyn, don't agree, I'm doing a course. (*She moves to Gayle*) It's your adrenaline level. It's gone berserk, my dear. Mine's the same. Our bodies are making pints of the stuff.
Martyn (*raising his voice as he insists*) Tell her it's the onions, Gayle!

Gayle still cries

Denise Now what you both have to realize is that selling up and moving out is one of the most stressful situations. I've cried almost every day since we put the house on the market. I usually have a drink when I'm having one of my turns. Where's that bottle?
Barrie Before we do … it might be a good idea if we sort out this little problem first. (*He takes a brass water tap from his trouser pocket*)
Gayle (*after a slight pause*) Is that my tap?
Barrie (*nodding*) One minute it was on the basin, the next it was in my hand.

Gayle tries desperately to control herself. Another roll of thunder

Martyn (*to Barrie*) You did turn the water off at the stopcock, didn't you?

Barrie starts to answer positively, then looks rather vague as he struggles to remember

   Gayle breaks down before rushing off into the kitchen

   Martyn runs off upstairs

Denise and Barrie look at each other

Barrie I think you were right all along, you know. They are a bit strange.
Denise Yes. It was obvious peeling onions wasn't responsible for all those tears. She's completely stressed out. Imagine what she'll be like when she finds out we're not going through with the sale of the house.
Barrie Wouldn't it be better to come straight out and tell them?
Denise You know it wouldn't. We've *signed*, remember. At the end of the

Act I

day, we've got to look after number one. If push came to shove, they could force us to sell and with our people backing out, we don't want that, do we?

Barrie It's a mess ... and all because you bought that book on how to do your own conveyancing.

Denise It's a very good book ... if two pages hadn't stuck together I'd never have missed the bit about, "When to exchange".

Barrie So we stick to plan A, then?

Denise Not sure. Never thought much of trying to put them off by charging for extras.

Barrie It was your idea.

Denise Best I could come up with at the time.

Barrie Well, we're not going to be able to do much about it tonight. They've got people coming, remember. Their purchasers.

Denise (*she has an idea*) That's it. Barrie, you're a genius.

Barrie I am?

Denise Yes, it's perfect. All we need do is change tactics.

Barrie doesn't quite follow

We don't try putting them off buying our place ... we try putting their people off buying this.

Barrie Right ... but how are we going to do that?

Denise Well, you are going to go upstairs and work alongside our little friend ... show him some of your DIY skills ... are you with me?

Barrie smiles and nods

And I in the meantime will practise my culinary and psychology skills in the kitchen.

Barrie Wonderful.

Denise By the time we've finished here tonight, no-one in their right mind would want to buy this place. Off you go.

Barrie See you in a bit.

Barrie goes off upstairs, rubbing his hands

Denise sighs before calling off into the kitchen

Denise (*calling*) Gayle? Would you like a hand out there?

Gayle (*off; snappily*) No, I'm fine!

Denise Now if that's not a cry for help, nothing is.

Denise eagerly marches off into the kitchen

Music

There is a pause, with no-one on stage. The Lights in Ray's living-room come up. It is a week later, Saturday evening. The weather is wonderful

When they appear, everyone is dressed differently from how they were before

Ray comes in from the garden

Dave and Di can be heard laughing off. Sheila shouts to them before coming inside

Sheila (*off; laughing*) Oh, give it a rest, will you?

Sheila comes in

Ray (*throwing a box of matches down on the bar*) I give up, I can't light the bloody thing.
Sheila It's twenty-five to bloody nine, Ray.
Ray (*a little irritable*) I know, I know ... don't keep on.
Sheila They're not goin' to come. I said they wouldn't. Not after wha' 'appened at their house last week.
Ray She's over tha' now, mun, or she wouldn't 'ave phoned you on Wednesday.
Sheila Yeah, but she didn't sound right.
Ray And they wouldn't have said they'd come tonight if they were 'oldin' a grudge.
Sheila They said they'd come tonight, Ray, cos they didn't want to say they wouldn't. Let's face it, you've buggered it all up. So much for tha' bloody scam of yours. (*She slaps him across the head*)
Ray They're only a bit late.
Sheila (*raising her voice*) An 'our and a 'alf?
Ray (*looking at his watch*) Well, if they don't come, they don't come ... we'll 'ave to find *another* 'ouse, tha's all.
Sheila You try tellin' Dave and Di tha'. All she keeps on 'bout is movin' in 'ere. They're goin' to play balls when they find out, I tell you.
Ray (*disappointed*) I was sure it was going to work out. I 'ad all the right vibes.
Sheila Lost everythin' now, we 'ave ... all because you wouldn't pay the full bloody price.
Ray We could 'ave done a lot with ten thousand pounds.
Sheila I *saw* myself in tha' 'ouse, Ray.

Dave and Di are heard laughing from the garden again

Act I

Ray How much 'ave those two 'ad to drink out there?
Sheila Loads, why?
Ray Come on ... better tell 'em and get it over with.

They are just about to leave for the garden when there is a knock on the front door. Both stop dead in their tracks, look at each other and laugh

Oh, I love it when a plan comes together.

He takes the matches and throws them at Sheila as she goes off into the garden

Go 'n' light the barbie, doll.

Sheila exits to the garden. Ray goes to answer the door

We hear voices off

(*Off*) Come in ... come in.

There's a crash, off

Yeah, mind the ladder.
Martyn (*off*) I'm sorry we're late.

Ray comes into his living-room, followed by Martyn and Gayle. They are not only dressed in different clothes but their whole demeanour is different. They both are much more vulnerable and are not nearly as confident as they appeared a week ago

Gayle (*entering*) You must have given us up by now.
Ray No, never gave it a thought, luv. Wha's an 'our and a 'alf between friends. Bugger all. Nothin' to go crackers 'bout. (*He realizes what he has said*) Oh, shit. Oh, sorry, Gayle. Oh, I could kick myself, ay.
Gayle That's all right.
Martyn Don't worry about it.
Ray 'Ow you feelin' now?
Gayle I'm fine.
Ray I'm glad to hear it. Me and Sheila were goin' to come and visit you, but when we realized you were in psychiatric ... well... Sheila got a thing 'bout them places. 'Er Granny's got Alzheimer's, see.
Gayle I wasn't hospitalised.
Ray (*finding it hard to believe*) Never ... well, *somebody* told Sheila you were.

Gayle I'm completely over it now.
Ray I'm sure you are, luv.
Gayle Completely.
Ray Well, I'm glad, since Sheila said I 'ad something to do with it.
Martyn Yes, well, I think you were the last straw.
Ray (*to Gayle*) But you're over it now, 'in' you?
Martyn Yes, and *I* think the whole episode did her a lot of good in the long run.
Ray Ay, well, when things build up inside like tha', it's all got to come out some'ow, 'asn't it? I was watchin' this programme on the telly the other night. We got Sky, see—but we're not takin' it with us … no. We're leavin' it. A gift, like. Wouldn't think of chargin' 'em for it. Anyway, they were showin' this volcano spewin' up all this muck? I said to Sheila, I said, "Gayle must 'ave felt like tha'," I said, "When we were over there last week".
Gayle (*after a slight pause*) Where is Sheila?
Ray In the garden. I've been tryin' for 'alf an 'our but can't do nothin' with it. She's goin' to 'ave a go at lightin' it now.
Martyn Lighting what?
Ray Didn't we tell you? We're not 'avin' a sit-down meal … not after what 'appened in *your* 'ouse last week … no. We're 'avin' a barbie out the back. Anyway, what are you having to drink?
Martyn We brought this. (*He holds out a bottle of wine*) Non-alcoholic. We thought it best under the circumstances. We don't want a repeat of what happened at our house.
Ray It wasn't *all* my fault, mind. Don't matter anyway, I've been on the Castlemaine Four X all afternoon.
Gayle Oh dear.
Ray (*assuring her*) No, I'm fine. You've got nothin' to worry 'bout, Gayle. (*Confidentially*) I'll be all right, luv, as long as I keep off the wine vinegar. (*He laughs hysterically. After quickly pulling himself together*) So wha' are you 'avin' to drink, then?
Gayle Just an orange juice for me.
Martyn And I'm driving, so I'll have a——
Sheila (*off*) Ray? Bring another can out, will you?
Ray (*calling to Sheila*) All right. (*To Martyn and Gayle*) I'll be back now.

Ray grabs a can of lager from the bar and goes out to the garden, leaving Martyn and Gayle alone for a moment

Martyn You all right?
Gayle Just don't leave me alone with him.
Martyn It'll be fine … don't panic. You are clear on everything now, are you?

Act I

Ray (*off*) I'll fetch 'em out now.
Martyn Just stick to what we agreed, right?
Gayle Right.

Ray returns and goes straight to the bar

Ray Now, then... Wha' are we 'avin' to drink?
Gayle Just an orange juice.
Martyn And I'll have a shandy.
Ray No! Nobody comes to *my* 'ouse and 'as a bloody shandy. And don't worry 'bout drivin' 'ome. Sheila's got you down for one of the spare bedrooms.
Gayle Oh, no ... no, we couldn't stay.
Ray It's all arranged, luv. You and Martyn are in one spare room, and Dave and Diane are in the other. (*He proceeds to pour drinks*)

Martyn and Gayle look at each other

Gayle (*almost afraid to ask*) Dave and Diane?
Ray Ay, they're out the back with Sheila... they're buyin' this 'ouse. You'll love Dave and Di, you will.
Gayle Sheila didn't say anything about anyone else being here.
Ray Didn't she? They're lookin' forward to meetin' you.
Gayle (*concerned*) Why?
Martyn You haven't said anything, have you? About, you know... (*He nods towards Gayle*) Last Friday night ... when you and Gayle ... you know.
Ray Oh, no ... nothin', no. We 'aven't said a word to anyone. 'Ere you are. (*He hands a drink to Martyn*) A Castlemaine for you. (*He hands a drink to Gayle*) And a gin and orange for you.
Gayle No, just an orange I said.
Ray Tha's right.
Gayle You said *gin* and orange.
Ray No, it's just orange. There's no gin, definitely.
Gayle Are you sure? I'm on medication. I can't drink alcohol.
Ray Honest. I squeezed it myself.
Martyn (*after a slight pause*) You're sure you haven't said anything to ... you know. (*He means Dave and Di*)
Ray Martyn, my old cock ... my lips are sealed.
Gayle I couldn't face it if anyone knew.
Ray You've got to get over it, mun. (*He pushes her*)
Gayle Yes ... well ... we'll stay for an hour ... but we won't be sleeping over. (*To Ray*) We've got to get up early in the morning... Martyn's niece is getting married at eleven o'clock and he's giving her away.
Ray There you are, then. I'll ring after and book you a taxi. Cheers.

Martyn and Gayle hesitantly sip their drink. Ray downs his in one

Suddenly male and female laughter is heard just off, and with a burst, Dave chases Di into the living-room. He is bare-chested and is wearing shorts and a pair of leather open sandals. Di is wearing a low-cut, ankle-length, cotton summer dress. He is squirting her with a water pistol as they both run around and past Martyn, Gayle and Ray. He eventually chases her back into the kitchen and presumably off out into the garden

Their laughter fades

He's a 'ell of a boy, 'in' he? You wouldn't believe he was a magistrate, would you?

Gayle immediately looks at Martyn

Just a joke...

Martyn and Gayle smile

He's a solicitor really. (*He laughs*) No, I'm windin' you up, mun. To be honest, he's only just come out ... he's done a bit of time.
Gayle (*physically stiffening*) You mean he's some sort of criminal?
Ray Ay, category B offender. Reformed now, of course.
Martyn (*almost afraid to ask*) What was he in prison for?
Ray Armed robbery.
Gayle (*after a slight pause*) And he's buying this place, you said?
Ray (*nodding*) First time buyer too.
Gayle Really?
Martyn Was he guilty?
Ray Well, he *said* he didn't do it, but he's payin' cash for this place.
Gayle (*she can hardly believe it*) *Cash?*
Ray Ay, there's no mortgage, nothin'.
Martyn He must have a lot of savings.
Ray Oh 'e 'as... Trouble is, it's other peoples. (*He laughs*) I wouldn't say anythin' 'bout it, though, if I were you.
Martyn I don't suppose he likes talking about it.
Ray Oh, he bloody *loves* talkin' 'bout it. Get 'im on to tha', and 'e won't talk 'bout nothin' else. He'll tell you 'ow 'e was framed, and 'ow 'e couldn't *possibly* 'ave done it because 'e was over 'ere with me playin' cards till four in the mornin'.
Gayle And was he?
Ray Was 'e 'ell.
Martyn You were his alibi.

Act I

Ray I didn't *want* to go to court or nothing, but...
Gayle You perjured yourself in front of a judge and jury?
Ray And the buggers didn't believe me. I got off with two years' probation and sixty 'ours community service.
Martyn What did *he* get?
Ray Six years ... but he came out after four for good behaviour.
Gayle He could have had you in prison with him asking you to lie. I'm not sure I'd want a friend like that.
Ray Oh, he's not my friend, he's my brother.

Sheila comes in from the garden. She has been working on the barbie and has finally got it to light... However her face is very smokey

Sheila Right, I've managed to get the barbie... (*She sees Martyn and Gayle*) Hiya Mart'... Gay' ... you came after all. (*To Gayle as she squeezes between them on the settee*) 'Ow are you feelin', luv?
Gayle Fine.
Sheila I didn't think you would, see. After you phoned I said to Ray, I said, "I don't think Gay' will come", I said. "She *still* sounds a bit bloody crackers to me" ... oh ... but you're better now.
Martyn Much.
Gayle It was only a *small* breakdown.
Sheila (*amazed*) Was it? Well, I'd 'ate to see you 'ave a big bugger, then.

Gayle fights not to cry

Oh, don't get upset now. I only said it to make you laugh. (*She presses her face to each side of Gayle's cheek*) I'm sorry.

As Sheila turns away, we see that she has left smoke marks from her own face on Gayle's

Ray When you can laugh 'bout somethin', you're over it, tha's wha' I say. And we can all 'ave a good laugh 'bout that Friday night at your 'ouse, can't we?

Everyone laughs in agreement except Gayle, who cries and gets up

Sheila (*shouting*) Ray, wha' the 'ell's the matter with you? (*To Gayle*) Come and sit down, Gayle. Honest to God, 'e's 'bout as sensitive as a bloody cactus tampon. (*To Gayle*) You sip up, luv.
Martyn There's only orange in there.
Sheila Well, tha's not good enough. Ray, get some gin.
Gayle No... I can't.

Sheila Nonsense. One's not goin' to 'urt you. (*Threatening*) Ray.

Ray reaches for the bottle of gin

Martyn She's on medication.
Gayle I'm on medication.
Sheila Well, it doesn't seem to be workin', love. Now wha' you need is a little somethin' to kick it into motion. (*She takes the bottle of gin from Ray and tops up Gayle's drink*) Now I don't want no arguments. You drink tha' up and I'm sure you'll feel a lot better.
Gayle I think I need to go to the bathroom.
Ray It's upstairs, luv.
Sheila If you're goin' to use the toilet, be careful. I've asked Ray to 'ave a look at the seat but it's like talkin' to the bloody wall.
Ray Wha' time 'ave I 'ad?
Sheila (*to Gayle*) It's a bit loose, see, and it's a bugger to pinch the inside of your leg if you're not careful.

Dave comes in from the garden, still with a water pistol

Dave (*threateningly*) Right, now I wan' everyone to stay calm and don't panic.

Everyone freezes. Martyn slowly puts his hands up in the air. Dave looks at him as if he's got two heads. Martyn immediately puts his hands down

Hey, Sheil', I don't know wha' you've done to tha' barbecue, Sheil', but the flames are so 'igh it almost cremated one of next door's pigeons.
Sheila It's all right... I put too much paraffin on it, I 'spect. Hey, wha's Di doin'?
Dave She's upset. She pinched the water gun and soaked me.
Sheila So wha's upset 'er?
Dave I pushed 'er in the pool.

They laugh

Gayle (*amazed*) You have a swimming pool?
Ray No, luv, just a fish pond, a couple of frogs and a newt, tha's all.
Sheila Ray, introduce everyone.
Ray Right, er ... this is Dave. Dave, this is Martyn and Gayle.
Dave *The* Martyn and Gayle? I've 'eard all about you.
Martyn Have you?
Gayle What?
Dave Ray was tellin' me 'bout last week when——

Act I   29

Ray (*to Dave, jumping in*) I've filled 'em in 'bout you, Dave... I thought I'd save you the bother, like.
Dave (*to Martyn and Gayle*) He's always stealin' my thunder.
Ray Yeah, well, at least you don't get time for doin' tha'.

They all laugh, Martyn and Gayle rather uncomfortably

Dave You've told 'em I've done a stretch, then?
Ray You didn't mind, did you?
Martyn (*looking nervous*) Four years ... that's a long time. I'm not sure Gayle would wait for *me* that long.
Dave Oh, Di's all right like tha' ... never missed a visit ... didn't know where I stashed the money, but she knew she'd be quids in once I got out.
Gayle (*almost afraid to ask*) So you were guilty, then?
Dave Oh, yeah, ay, but I don't tell everyone, mind. (*Almost threateningly*) And I know *you* won't say nothin' ... will you?

Gayle shakes her head until it almost comes off

Martyn I've never met anyone who's been inside.
Dave Shame I got out when I did, in a way. The BBC were goin' to do a "Rough Justice", on me. I'd 'ave got off and sued the state for thousands.
Gayle But you were guilty, you said.
Dave So? It didn't stop the others.

Suddenly Di appears just inside the doorway. She is dripping wet

Di (*looking for Dave*) Where is he? I'm goin' to get you for this.
Dave There she is, the light of my life.
Di You've ruined this dress.
Dave I was goin' to rip it off you after anyway. (*To Martyn*) I haven't given 'er a night off since I come out.
Di You'll 'ave to dredge the pond, Ray, I've lost one of my shoes.
Dave Di, this is Martyn and Gayle.
Di Who?
Ray Martyn and Gayle, you know.
Di Oh, right... 'ello... (*To Gayle as she remembers*) Yes. You're the one who last Friday——

Sheila jumps in

Sheila Di, come on... I'd better find you somethin' to change into. (*She starts to lead Di off upstairs*)
Di Gayle, that's the one that went crackers, innit?

Sheila and Di leave

Dave She's a good sport.
Gayle If Martyn did anything like that to me——
Dave You'd 'ave a nervous breakdown. (*He laughs*)
Gayle (*upset*) He knows... (*To Martyn*) He knows...
Ray All I said was——
Gayle (*insisting*) You said you hadn't told anyone.
Martyn (*agreeing*) That's right. "Martyn, my old cock", you said, "my lips are sealed".
Gayle (*crying*) I wouldn't have come if I knew you'd told——
Ray Dave isn't goin' to say anythin', mun ... and who'd believe 'im if he did?
Dave Tha's right. I could 'ardly believe it myself when 'e told me.

Gayle begins to cry

Mind you, we've 'ad a good old laugh about it since, 'aven't we, Ray?

Gayle cries even more

Gayle I'm going to have to go to the bathroom.

It's all proving too much for Gayle and she rushes off upstairs

Ray is about to go after her

Martyn No, leave 'er. She'll be all right.
Ray But...
Martyn Best for 'er 'ave five minutes to 'erself. You see, she still feels a bit raw about things.
Ray (*hesitantly*) Well, if you think that's best.
Martyn Yes, I think so.
Ray Another drink, then. (*He sorts out the drinks*)
Martyn No, not for me, thanks.
Ray Dave?
Dave Ay.
Ray (*handing him a can*) You are.

A slight pause

Dave (*to Martyn*) House still on the market, then, is it?
Martyn Yes, yes, it's still up for sale.
Ray (*to Martyn*) No 'ard feelin's?

Act I

Martyn No... none at all... Well, we wouldn't be here tonight if there was.
Ray Tha's wha' I was thinkin', like. We'd 'ave still gone a'ead and bought your place, see ... but, well, you saw the survey, if only you'd come down tha' ten grand.
Martyn (*to Ray, tentatively*) Yes, well, I'm sure you'll find another place pretty soon now.
Ray Ay, we 'ave, yeah. Put an offer in this mornin' for a smashin' little bungalow. Big enough for me and Sheil', see. (*He hands Martyn a lager. He turns, and as he hands a lager to Dave, he winks at him*)
Martyn Oh, I see ... well, er ... congratulations.
Ray Yes. (*He toasts*) Cheers, everybody. 'Ere's to a successful move. And to you too, Martyn ... when you find another buyer, like.
Martyn Oh ... cheers.

Ray and Dave drink up

Ray Right, then! Let's go out to this barbie. (*He puts his arms around Martyn and Dave and heads for the garden*)

Suddenly the doorbell rings. Ray stops

Who the 'ell is tha' now? (*To Dave and Martyn*) You go outside, you two. I'll be with you in a minute.

Dave and Martyn start to leave, but at the back door Dave turns to Martyn

Dave Hey, Martyn...

Martyn turns to look at him and Dave squirts him in the face with the water pistol

Dave laughs and walks off

Ray goes off to answer the front door

Martyn follows Dave out

Mumbled voices are heard off before someone is heard crashing into the ladders

Ray (*off*) Yeah, mind the ladders.

Denise comes in, followed by Ray

Denise Not a bad time, is it?
Ray Well, yes. (*A little anxious*) We're not supposed to meet till Monday.
Denise Won't be here. (*Lying*) Barrie and I are popping off for the week. Need to get away for a while.
Ray He's not with you tonight, then.
Denise Waiting outside in the car.
Ray Did you bring the money?
Denise Three thousand pounds ... cash! (*She slaps it down on the bar*)

Ray quickly picks it up and puts it in his pocket

Aren't you going to count it?
Ray I trust you.
Denise Well, I don't trust *you*. Sign this. (*She slaps a document down on the bar*)
Ray Wha' is it?
Denise An agreement. I'm not stupid enough to hand over that kind of money without a signature.
Ray Some sort of receipt, is it?
Denise (*taking a pen out of her bag and placing it on the document*) It's a document confirming that you will not under any circumstances be going ahead with the purchase of the Walshes' house.
Ray (*a bit jittery because the Walshes are in the house*) Oh, right.
Denise We have to have some sort of assurance. (*She nods for him to sign*)

He signs. She picks it up to check it, and is happy that everything is in order

Now, if you'll just let me have the survey.
Ray Wha'?
Denise The survey you had done on the Walshes' property.
Ray Wha' you want tha' for?
Denise I have to have proof of the state of the place.
Ray (*lying*) I don't know where it is.
Denise Well, in that case I'll have my money back.
Ray Oh, look, there it is by there. (*He takes a brown envelope from behind the bar and hands it to her*)
Denise And remember, you've just signed a legally binding document. I'll see myself out.

Denise goes, closing the door behind her

Ray kisses the wad of money before putting it in his pocket and going out into the garden

Act I 33

The action now moves back to last Friday

The door chimes in the Walshes' part

Music

   Gayle, (who is not now wearing an apron), comes out of the kitchen and answers the front door

Gayle (*off; sounding absolutely delighted*) Oh, hallo... Come in. Isn't it a dreadful night?
Sheila (*off*) I 'ope we're not late or nothin'.
Gayle (*off*) No, no, no ... no, you're fine. Go through. Ray not with you?

   A very wet Sheila comes into the room. She stands, dripping, holding a bottle of wine vinegar

   Gayle enters

Sheila He is comin' ... he's tryin' to park the bloody car. A bottle of wine for you.
Gayle (*taking it*) Oh, thank you very much. Let me take your coat. (*She helps her off with it*) I'll hang it up.
Sheila It's only an old one ... chuck it on the back of a chair.

   Denise appears from the kitchen, wearing the apron

Denise That green stuff you're cooking ... it's looking very sad.
Gayle (*trying to control herself*) Sheila, this is Denise.
Sheila Friends?
Gayle Yes ... no ... yes... We're buying her house.
Sheila Well, tha's a coincidence, innit? And I'm buyin' yours off you.

Slight pause

   Ooh, somethin' smells nice. I'm lookin' forward to the food, I 'aven't eaten nothin' all day, so I 'ope there's plenty of it.
Denise You're having guests.
Gayle Well...
Denise You should have said.
Gayle It's not a problem.
Denise Afraid it is, dear. Coats?
Sheila S'cuse me, d' you think per'aps——

Gayle There's no need to leave.
Sheila I don't want to bother you, but——
Denise Couldn't possibly put on you.
Gayle It's fine, honestly.
Denise Absolutely no way to stay now.
Gayle Oh, very well, then.

Denise draws breath, then realises she has talked herself out of it

Denise *(after a slight pause)* Oh... Right.
Sheila *(after a slight pause)* Any chance of a towel or somethin', I'm bloody marinatin' by 'ere. *(She laughs)*
Gayle I'll get you one. Excuse me.

Gayle goes off upstairs

A roll of thunder. A slight pause

Sheila Bloody awful night, innit?
Denise She's not at all well, you know.
Sheila Gayle?

Denise nods

Wha's the matter with 'er?
Denise Between you and I, she's on the verge.
Sheila Is she? *(After a slight pause)* On the verge of wha', then?
Denise She's about to explode, and in my opinion it's not going to take very much.
Sheila *(thinking about it for a brief second)* It's the time of the month, I 'spect. I'm the same, see. Ray reckons it's like livin' with a ravin' bloody banshee one week in four.
Denise I don't think it has anything to do with the menstrual cycle.
Sheila We 'aven't got kids yet. He offered to pay for me to go 'n' 'ave my tubes blown. "You bugger off", I said. This is comin' from a man now who refused point blank to 'ave 'is ear syringed.

Ray appears at the door

Ray Are you talkin' about me?
Sheila But 'e can 'ear what 'e wants to as you can see. *(She laughs)* 'Ow are you so wet?
Ray Well, it's still rainin' innit. I 'ad to put the car at the end of the street 'cause some silly bugger's parked up the drive.

Act I

Sheila Ray, this is ... I'm sorry, luv, I've forgot who you are now.
Denise Denise. Denise Lovejoy.
Ray 'Ow are you, luv. It's terrible out there. Where is everybody?
Sheila Well, Gayle's gone to fetch a towel.
Denise And Barrie and Martyn are upstairs. A slight problem in the bathroom.
Ray (*with suspicious interest*) Oh, ay. (*He waits for a further explanation*)
Denise (*eventually*) It's the taps ... loose or something. Barrie, that's my husband, he'll have everything under control.
Ray Plumber, then, is 'e?
Denise No, but he does work for the Water Authority.

Sheila and Ray look at each other

He *started* on the manual side and worked his way into management.
Sheila A white-collar worker, then?
Denise Oh, yes.
Ray *I* wear a white collar to work.
Sheila It's not the same though, Ray.
Ray It's near enough.
Denise What do you do?
Sheila He works in a slaughter 'ouse.
Denise Management?
Ray I kill cows.
Sheila It's nothin' clever.
Ray It's a very important job, I'll 'ave you know, 'specially since this BSE thing. One slip from me and the whole market could be flooded with offal. (*To Denise*) You 'aving dinner 'ere tonight, eh?
Sheila She was, (*to Denise*) but you're goin' 'ome now, Den, 'in' you, you said.
Denise Had no idea they were expecting company.
Ray Company? It's only us, mun.
Denise We'll be leaving shortly, just as soon as Barrie's fixed the tap.
Ray Excuse me, are you aware of anythin' else tha's wrong with the place?
Sheila Not now, Ray.
Ray No, no, if you don't ask you don't find out. (*To Denise*) We're buyin' this place, see, and the thing is ... we've paid a lot of money and 'ad a survey done and to be honest, it pulls this place to pieces.
Denise (*very interested*) Really?
Ray We feel awful about it, don't we, Sheil'? (*To Denise*) She's got 'er 'eart set on movin' to this place, see.
Denise What did the survey say exactly? Are there major defects?
Ray Risin' damp, subsidence——

Denise Subsidence? So you've been refused a mortgage?
Ray Er, no... (*Lying*) They've offered so much, like. Either we make up the difference ourselves, or come to an arrangement with the vendors.
Denise (*fishing*) Not too much of a problem, then.
Sheila It is for us, we 'aven't got it.
Ray And we feel awful 'bout it, you know...
Sheila And we don't *want* to be the one to break the chain, but...

Denise turns her head away. This piece of information is obviously good news for her. A slight pause

Ray Well, don't let's be negative. Who knows, maybe they can come up with the difference.
Sheila I doubt whether they've got *tha'* kind of money, Ray.
Denise How much is it?
Ray (*immediately*) Ten grand, luv.

Gayle comes back in with a towel. She looks gob-smacked and stressed

Denise (*on seeing Gayle*) Problem, dear? You look dreadful.
Sheila Is tha' for me? (*She takes the towel from Gayle*)
Gayle (*barely able to speak*) I can't believe it. Not tonight of all nights.
Denise (*leading her to the sofa*) Come and sit down.
Ray (*to Gayle*) How are you, luv? (*To Sheila*) She looks awful. I'll get 'er a drink.
Denise What is it? Something wrong?
Gayle I went to get a towel... I thought I was seeing things.
Ray Wha' you fancy, Gayle? Whisky, gin, or a nice drop of wine.
Sheila Pour 'er a glass of the one *I* fetched.
Ray Anyone else?
Denise No, not for me.
Ray Sheila?
Sheila I'll 'ave a gin, I will.
Denise (*to Gayle*) You were saying ... upstairs.
Gayle What's all this carpet on the landing, I thought. When I looked, they've taken up the floor in the bathroom. (*On the verge of tears*) There's copper piping everywhere.
Denise That's Barrie for you. If nothing else, he's thorough.
Gayle He was only supposed to put the tap back on.
Denise Now you mustn't get upset. He's a perfectionist.
Ray 'Ere you are, luv. (*He hands her a glass of wine vinegar*)
Gayle (*taking it but not drinking it yet*) "What's that in my bath", I asked. No-one answered me, but I demanded to know, "What is my combination boiler doing face down in the bath?"

Act I

Ray pours himself a drink

Denise He's probably giving it some sort of service.
Gayle Do you think I could have a cigarette?
Sheila I've got a fag ... 'ave one of mine. (*She takes out a cigarette and gives one to Gayle*) Anyone else? Den?
Denise I don't.
Sheila Ray?
Ray I'll 'ave one of my own now. (*But he doesn't ... not yet*)

Sheila lights Gayle's cigarette. Gayle drags long and hard, looking like she very much needed a shot of nicotine

>(*Standing with a glass in one hand and a bottle of something in the other*) So ... there's some sort of fault with your central 'eating system, then, is there?

Gayle (*insisting*) No, there's not! There's nothing wrong with it ... there's never been anything wrong with it. It has a full service history.
Denise Well, Barrie wouldn't take it apart for no reason. Whatever's wrong, he'll have it fixed in no time. A real wizard like that.
Gayle I hope you're right.
Denise Trust me. (*She pauses slightly*) Well, love to stay talking, but I have things to do in the kitchen.
Gayle (*remembering*) My God, the food. (*She attempts to stand up*)

Denise forces her back down

Denise Don't worry ... leave it to me. Everything's under control.
Gayle Are you sure? I thought you weren't———
Denise If I can cook for eighty-five Girl Guides on an open fire in the rain, I can rustle up a little something for us lot, believe me. (*She makes for the kitchen*)
Sheila Sorry, but I've got to see this.
Denise Then come along, Brown Owl.

Denise marches off into the kitchen and Sheila follows

A slight pause in which Gayle takes another long much-needed drag on her cigarette

Ray Hold on to your seat-belts, it's goin' to be a bumpy night.

Another roll of thunder

Gayle (*trying to be positive*) I'm not concerned… I'm not… I'm not worried about a *thing*. (*She obviously is*)
Ray There you are, then.
Gayle And at least you'll know before we exchange contracts that everything is in perfect working order.
Ray Oh, there you are, then.
Gayle As for the food … if the worst comes to the worst we can send out … an Indian or something.
Ray (*rubbing his stomach*) I don't think I could take a chance on an Indian tonight, Gayle … or Sheila either for tha' matter.
Sheila (*off*) Oh, bloody 'ell, wha' are you goin' to do now, Den?
Denise (*off*) It's all right … don't panic … it's probably only temporary.

Gayle and Ray look at each other

Sheila pops her head around the kitchen door

Sheila (*to Gayle*) You're not 'aving much luck tonight, luv, are you?
Ray Wha's the matter now?
Sheila There's no gas comin' through to the cooker. Probably switched it off at the main.
Denise (*off*) It's all right, there's a microwave here.
Sheila Dib dib dib.

Sheila disappears back into the kitchen

Ray (*to Gayle*) Saved by the bell by there, then.
Gayle Not really, there's no plug on it.
Ray No problem, Sheila changes *all* ours in our 'ouse. She knows 'lectrics like the back of 'er 'and.
Sheila (*off*) You sure you can change a plug now, Den?
Denise (*off*) Heavens, yes.
Sheila (*off*) Only, I can do it, see.
Denise (*off*) I'm quite capable, thank you.
Gayle I had it all worked out. Tonight was going to be perfect.
Ray Ah, well, best laid plans an' all.
Gayle I was cooking a beautiful meal. (*She waits for him to ask what, to no avail. She is left eventually to say*) Épinards à la Niçoise.
Ray There you are, then. Don't worry 'bout it. They'll sort somethin' out now between 'em.

Barrie comes in from upstairs, carrying a radiator

Barrie You're never going to believe this.

Act I

Ray and Gayle turn to see him

Gayle (*she can't believe her eyes*) What's going on?
Barrie Everything's under control.
Gayle What are you doing with that radiator?
Barrie Now I'm glad you asked that. (*To Ray*) Oh, hallo, we haven't met.
Ray Ray.
Barrie Barrie.

They shake hands

Gayle The radiator. What are you doing with it?
Barrie It needed bleeding.
Gayle I might be a woman, but even I know you don't have to take if off the wall for that.
Barrie Sod's law, I'm afraid. Didn't have an Allen key. Have to drain off the whole lot now. Couldn't tip it down the hand basin because ... well, you don't need to know that at the moment.
Gayle (*trying to control herself*) I'm not being funny... I'm not being funny or anything, but I want that radiator back on the bathroom wall immediately.
Barrie Oh, I can't do that.
Gayle Why not?
Barrie Because it's from your bedroom. Bleed one, bleed them all. Excuse me.

Barrie carries the radiator off into the kitchen

Gayle closes her eyes and starts to cry... Physically

In the Gibbon part, we move forward to the following Saturday—the Walshes' side remains set on Friday the previous week

Sheila and Di come in from upstairs. Di is now wearing something of Sheila's which looks quite silly on her. Sheila is carrying Di's dirty clothes

Ray (*to Gayle*) I know this might not be the right time or anythin' ... but I've got a bit of bad news. It's not lookin' very good. In fact it's lookin' sick, luv.
Di (*to Sheila*) When do you think we'll be moving in here?
Sheila It depends. Ray's playing a blinder.
Ray It's a bit embarrassin' really. Per'aps if I was to show it to you. (*He takes an envelope from his inside pocket*)
Sheila If 'e pulls it off, we could all be on the move sooner than we think. (*She hands Di her glass and she drinks*) Cheers.

Ray (*hesitating*) Or on the other 'and maybe Martyn would be my best bet.
Di (*really excited*) I'm packed already.
Ray After all, what would you know 'bout risin' damp and underpinning?
Gayle Underpinning?
Ray It's just a fancy word for "reinforcin' the foundations".
Sheila (*confidentially*) Only I've got to watch wha' I'm sayin' because…
Gayle (*almost dazed*) Reinforcing the foundations?
Sheila Because the last thing I want is for Martyn and Gayle to catch on.
Ray Sounds awful, don't it, and it *is* … but it can be fixed, like. Expensive it is.

Dave comes in from the garden in the Gibbon part

Dave Hey, Sheil', got any beefburgers?
Sheila On a tray out the back.
Dave (*shaking his head*) The birds 'ave shit all over 'em.
Sheila Didn't Ray cover 'em up? I bloody kill 'im, I will. There's a pack of twenty-four in the freezer. I'll get 'em now.

Sheila goes off to the kitchen

Dave goes out to the garden

The following two lines are pre-recorded, as though spoken in the Walsh kitchen

(*Off*) Blue wire to the left, brown to the right.
Denise (*off*) I know, I know.
Ray Now as *I* see it you've got two options. You can drop ten grand and I'll get one of my contacts to sort it, or you can stick to the price and do the job *yourself*. Providin' there's nothin' else wrong, of course.

Gayle thinks about this

In the Gibbon part, Sheila comes in from the kitchen with a frozen packet of beefburgers

Sheila I've 'ad a gutsful of those pigeons. I fell asleep out the back last week and when I woke up I 'ad one on each shoulder. You should 'ave seen 'em, they were everywhere … there was more shit on me than on Nelson's Column.

Sheila and Di laugh

Act I

Gayle (*almost afraid to ask*) How much is it all going to cost?
Ray (*immediately*) Ten grand, luv.

Barrie enters from the Walshes' kitchen with the radiator and takes it upstairs

I'm sorry to be the bearer of bad tidin's, you know...
Di Tell me about this blinder of Ray's, then.
Ray I mean, we felt awful ourselves when we read the survey.
Sheila He came up with this idea to knock ten grand off the price, didn't 'e?
Ray We'd meet you 'alf way, of course, but we 'aven't got tha' kind of cash, see. But don't worry, I'll 'ave a word with Martyn ... see wha' 'e can sort out.
Sheila If 'e can pull the wool, I'm 'avin' a little runaround. Come on, let's go out the back with the others.

Just as Sheila is about to leave with Di and the beefburgers, Martyn comes into the room

(*Seeing Martyn*) Oh, we were just comin' out to the garden.
Martyn Looking for Gayle, I am.
Sheila Isn't she out there with you?
Martyn She went to the bathroom.
Sheila Must be still in there, then. (*To Di*) Come on. Don't be long now, Mart'. Bit of luck we'll be eatin' in twenty minutes.

Sheila and Di go

Martyn (*calling upstairs*) Gayle? Everything all right up there?

Martyn goes off upstairs

Ray It's a funny old business, inn't it ... sellin' a 'ouse. (*After a slight pause*) They say it's up there in the stress level with death and divorce, see. Mind, I don't get stressed myself. I bet you suffer from stomach ulcers, don't you?
Gayle No, but I think I might be having one soon.
Ray I 'ope I 'aven't gone and spoiled tonight for you now.
Gayle Well, not single-handedly, you haven't.
Ray *I* feel pretty confident 'bout it all, I do.
Gayle Oh, there you are, then.
Ray I've told you 'bout the survey. Whatever 'appens now won't seem so bad.

Barrie comes in from upstairs, carrying a copper water boiler

Barrie Sorry about this.
Gayle (*on seeing him*) Oh God, no!
Barrie Martyn mentioned the immersion heater?
Gayle (*screaming*) Martyn!

Martyn rushes in from upstairs, in the Walshes' part

Martyn (*to Gayle*) Sorry, Gayle, sorry. I happened to mention…
Ray Let's *all* 'ave a drink, is it? (*He pours several glasses during the following*)
Martyn He had it out of the airing cupboard before I had time to blink.
Barrie It's redundant … you don't need it. Not with a combination boiler.
Gayle Have you put it back? The boiler?
Barrie My next job.

Sheila comes in from the Walshes' kitchen

Sheila Hey Gay', do you know your oven door don't shut tidy?
Barrie A two minute job, that.
Gayle (*absolutely desperate*) Martyn?
Martyn It's all right, sweetheart.
Sheila And I only went to open the kitchen window, look… (*She holds up a shiny gold handle from the double-glazed window*)
Gayle I think I want to die.
Barrie If you've got the screw, I can put that back straight away.
Gayle (*upset and shouting*) Send them home, Martyn … send them home…
Martyn (*to everyone*) Perhaps it would be better under the circumstances.
Sheila Home? I 'aven't 'ad bugger all to eat yet.
Barrie Give me ten minutes and I can have everything sorted.
Gayle (*screaming*) Martyn!
Ray (*shouting*) Calm down!

Everyone goes quiet except Gayle who is breathing fast and heavy

(*Shouting*) Nobody's goin' anywhere, right? (*Quieter now*) Not yet anyway. Gayle… I give you my word, and it's as good as my bond——
Sheila It is, yeah, fair play, I've got to say.
Ray I give you my word tha' I will personally see tha' Barrie by 'ere, will 'ave everythin' back as 'e found it——
Martyn Yes, but when?
Ray Just as soon as we've all calmed down and 'ad a drink. (*He shouts again*) Right? Now is tha' fair enough?

No-one answers

Act I

(*Quieter*) Right. (*He hands Barrie, Martyn and Sheila a glass of wine. He then calls to Denise out in the kitchen*) Are you goin' to join us, er ... wha's a name now?
Barrie Denise.
Ray (*calling to her*) Denise?
Denise (*off*) Be with you in a tick. Just plugging in the micro.
Ray Drinks. (*He hands a glass of wine to everyone*) Here's to a great night for everyone. Cheers!

They raise their glasses and drink

Denise (*off; shouting*) Here we go!

Everyone immediately sprays out the wine

Ray Shit...! It's bastard vinegar!

Suddenly there is a flash from the kitchen. Black-out

Music

ACT II

The same. A short while later

There is a huge roll of thunder as the house lights dim and opening music plays. Lights come up on the Gibbons' half of the stage only, although there is no-one in either living-room. Voices are heard off in the Walshes' kitchen

Martyn feels his way in from the hallway. He is followed by Gayle

Martyn (*trying to re-assure her*) Of course there aren't any evil forces afoot. It's a fuse, for God's sake. We won't be in the dark for long.
Denise (*off*) Are you sure, dear? Try again. I always keep a few candles in *my* kitchen.
Sheila (*off*) But it's not my kitchen, is it? I don't even know what bloody cupboard I'm in.

Suddenly there's one almighty crash of pots and pans

Denise (*off*) I think you're in with the saucepans, dear.
Martyn The sooner I find the fuse wire, the sooner Barrie can fix it.
Gayle (*panicking*) No, you mustn't.
Martyn What?
Gayle Let Barrie anywhere near the fuse-box.
Martyn I'm sure he knows what he's doing.
Gayle Martyn, how can you say that after he's practically dismantled our combination boiler?
Martyn He can put that back in two minutes, he said. He didn't intend servicing it, it's just that one thing lead to another. Now you sit there and don't panic. Everything is under control. (*He walks straight into a wall*) It'll be plain sailing once we have the lights back on. Now, fuse wire. (*He feels his way to the downstage cabinet*)

Sheila has felt her way to the living-room door

Sheila I thought I 'eard voices.
Martyn Sheila ... how are you?
Sheila (*amazed*) God! 'Ow did you know it was me?

Act II

Martyn Oh, I'd recognize those dulcet tones anywhere.
Sheila Says 'e with 'is silver tongue. 'Ow long are we goin' to be in the bloody dark?
Martyn We won't be too long now, once I've found the fuse wire. How are things in the kitchen, is it?
Sheila Well, apart from the fact tha' there's no gas or 'lectric in there, and you can't see a 'and in front of you, everythin's fine.
Gayle (*almost afraid to ask*) How are the épinards?
Sheila Were they those green stuffed cabbage things?
Gayle Were?
Sheila They're in the bin, luv. Denise said they looked like a pile of sheep shit ... only she didn't say shit, she said "Menno".

On hearing that piece of news, Gayle bangs her head several times on the arm of the sofa

What's tha' noise?
Martyn Gayle? Is that you?

She doesn't answer. She just continues to head-bang the arm

(*Stumbling over in her direction*) Gayle, now you've got to pull yourself together. It's not as bad as it seems.
Sheila Course it's not...
Martyn I mean, I know you invited people round for a candle-lit dinner——
Sheila But it's not your fault if you 'aven't got any bloody candles, love.
Martyn You're probably feeling terribly embarrassed by it, aren't you?
Sheila (*sitting next to Gayle on the sofa*) But no-one's goin' to laugh 'bout it be'ind your back, mun.
Martyn That's right. I mean, *you're* not going to say anything to anyone, Sheila, are you?

Gayle stops banging her head

Sheila Me? My lips are sealed, luv. Anyway, I'd feel soft *myself* tellin' people you asked me round for a slap-up meal and ended up 'avin' beans on toast. (*She feels her way to the sofa*) I'll 'ave to 'ave somethin' to eat soon though, mind, I'm beginin' to feel a bit funny. Light-'eaded like.

Martyn reaches out and takes Sheila by the arm, thinking it's Gayle

Martyn Well, there's nothing you can do down here for a minute... (*He helps her to her feet*) Why don't you come upstairs and have a little lay down. You might feel a bit better, then.

Martyn helps Sheila out of the room, but doesn't exit himself

In the Gibbons' part, set on the following Saturday as before, Ray and Dave come in from the garden

Dave Just as long as you know that if anything goes wrong with this deal, it's your *neck*. I mean it. This deal go sour an' Di will kill me ... but not before I've killed you first, right? You want to get that Martyn and Gayle down, Ray, cos they're no good to any of us up there.

Ray Look, tha' Gayle, she's a wreck, 'in' she ... and tha's just 'ow I want 'er. If I've timed it right, she'll peak tonight and be ready to agree to drop tha' ten grand.

In his living-room, Martin speaks to Gayle, thinking she is Sheila

Martyn (*sighing*) You know, Sheila, I wonder sometimes if Gayle needs some sort of professional help.

Gayle looks outraged

Dave I don't know why you don't pay the full askin' price.
Ray Hey ... ten grand's ten grand.
Martyn She's always been a bit neurotic.
Dave I'm lending you the money, 'in' I?
Ray I know, but, don't go tellin' *them* tha'. They still think I'm 'avin' a mortgage.
Martyn It's just she can get the wrong side of hysterical sometimes.
Dave I'd still get 'em down if I were you. If she's a wreck like you said, you could run the risk of 'er committin' 'arri-carri in your bathroom.
Martyn Between you and me, Sheila, I've had my share of problems with Gayle.
Dave What you've got to remember is, you're not dealin' with a normal person 'ere, are you?
Martyn She has been known to, er ... well, you know.
Ray No, but she's not as bad as *tha'*.
Dave We *are* talkin' 'bout the same woman, are we?
Martyn Who would think, to look at her, she'd be capable of ... well... But listen, you won't mention it to her, will you? It's just that I don't think Gayle would appreciate it if she knew I'd confided in you.

Di comes in from the Gibbon garden

Di I thought this party was supposed to be al frisco.

Act II

Martyn I've told you this because...
Di Sheila wants you a minute, Ray.
Martyn Well, because, you might understand Gayle a bit better——
Ray Me?
Martyn And see her in a different light so to speak.
Di (*sitting on the sofa*) "Tell the piss-head I want him", she said.
Ray And you tell 'er I'll be there when I'm ready.
Martyn (*remembering*) Light. Fuse wire. My God. (*He feels his way back to the cabinet*)
Ray The days are long gone when I jump when *she* calls.
Sheila (*off*) Ray!

Ray makes a hasty exit out into the garden

Di (*laughing*) Well, she's got *him* where she wants him.
Dave (*advancing towards her*) And I know exactly where I want *you*. (*He dives on to the sofa on top of her*)
Di Oh, give it a rest, Dave, will you? We've been like a pair of rabbits since you got out. I won't be able to walk tidy, you keep this up.
Dave Well, I've missed you, 'aven't I.
Di I've missed you too, but we're not shagging for Wales.
Dave Well, nobody told me. (*He gets off her*)
Di Cool 'ead now and keep somethin' for after. (*She winks at him*)
Dave (*smiling*) Oh, right.

Di goes towards the hall door

Where you goin'?
Di Bathroom. I need a pee.
Dave You won't get in.

She stops and looks at him

Tha' Gayle's in there 'avin' a breakdown.
Di Well, I'm bustin', I've got to do it *somewhere*.
Dave I've told Ray he's got to get her out or he'll never make the deal.
Di He's got to crack it tonight, Dave. (*Absolutely determined*) I'm not livin' out of cardboard boxes much longer.
Dave I 'ave told 'im.
Di Well, put pressure on him. (*Beat*) If I don't go soon, I'm goin' to do myself an injury.
Dave Hang on... I'll sort somethin' out for you now. (*He heads for the kitchen*)

Di Where you off?
Dave Just keep your legs crossed.

Dave goes out to the kitchen

Ray is heard from the kitchen in the Walshes' part

Ray (*off*) Oi, Martyn, any luck with tha' fuse wire?
Martyn (*calling off*) I've definitely got some somewhere.
Ray (*off*) I'd 'urry up and find it, if I were you. Barrie's talkin' 'bout rewirein' out 'ere.

Gayle almost collapses on the sofa

Martyn If I've asked Gayle once, I've asked her a thousand times to clean out these drawers.

In the Gibbon house, Di begins to walk around the room with her legs squeezed tightly together

Di Hurry up, Dave, will you.
Ray (*off*) No, leave the porch door alone, Barrie, for God's sake, will you?

Gayle gets up from the sofa and feels her way toward the hallway

(*Off*) It's dangerous, mun. I wouldn't take the glass out now ... not in the dark!
Martyn (*finding the wire*) Got it. (*He calls*) I've got it!

Ray feels his way into the room as Gayle is feeling her way out

Ray You got it?
Martyn I knew I had some somewhere.
Ray Where is it? (*He tentatively walks* DCL *in front of the sofa*)
Martyn Here. (*He tentatively walks* US *behind the sofa*)
Ray Martyn?
Martyn Ray?
Ray Where you by?
Martyn Here, by the settee.

Barrie feels his way into the room

Ray finds the settee. He starts to the left of it

Act II

Ray Right. I've got the settee.
Martyn Now, then ... follow the tone of my voice. I am here, where are you?

They cross with their arms outstretched, one behind the sofa and one in front of it. They miss each other

Ray Martyn? Stop playing silly buggers, mun. Where are you?

Martyn bumps into Barrie and thinks he's Ray

Martyn There you are. (*He places the fuse wire into Barrie's hand and moves off*) Shouldn't be long now.

Ray bumps into Barrie and thinks it's Martyn

Ray Good. (*He takes the fuse wire from Barrie*) Right. I'll go 'n' take it to Barrie. (*He is about to feel his way out of the room*)
Barrie I am Barrie.
Ray Oh. 'Ere you are, then. (*He waves the fuse wire around in the air*)

Barrie does the same with his hands and eventually they meet up and Barrie gets the wire

Right, Sparky, off you go.
Martyn I still don't know how you're going to change a fuse in the dark.
Barrie Piece of cake. It's all a matter of touch.

Barrie turns and crashes into the cabinet at the back before leaving the room

Di (*calling*) Dave, hurry up, I've only got one pair of knickers.
Martyn (*standing next to Ray behind the sofa*) Between you and me, Ray, Gayle's half convinced someone's putting the mockers on tonight.
Ray Is she?
Martyn I've told her not to be ridiculous, but...
Ray Now who would want to do a thing like tha'?
Martyn But to be honest, I'm beginning to wonder myself now.
Ray *I* think it's all a bit of a laugh, I do.
Martyn It's turning into a nightmare.
Ray From your point of view, I s'pose it is.
Martyn You see, it's just that Gayle can't cope very well when things go wrong.
Ray And I don't suppose me givin' 'er the bad news 'bout the survey 'elped.

Martyn Gayle hasn't mentioned any bad news.
Ray Hasn't she? Sheila 'as 'ad a word with her, then, 'as she?
Martyn No.
Ray Well, she was in 'ere with 'er five minutes ago. You sent 'er upstairs to lay down.
Martyn No, I sent *Gayle* upstairs to lay… (*He realizes what he has done*) Oh God … what have I done? What have I said? She'll kill me.
Ray No, Sheila never takes offence.
Martyn Gayle? Are you here now, my love?

Martyn feels his way out of the room and off into the hallway

Ray is left laughing as he feels his way to the drinks cabinet

On the Gibbon side, Dave comes back in with a milk bottle and holds it towards Di

Dave Right, 'ow's tha'?
Di I can't go in tha', I'd miss.
Dave Hey, you can use this, look. (*He reaches for the ice bucket on the bar*) Come on. Beggars can't be choosers.
Di Wha' if someone was to come in?
Dave I'll stand guard.

She hesitates but he insists

Go on. You could 'ave done it by the time you've been immin' and arrin'.

Reluctantly Di gives in

Di Make sure you keep an eye out, then, right? (*She takes the bucket from the drinks bar. She raises her dress and sits on the rather small bucket. She sits in a way that the bucket and her legs cannot be seen under her*)

Dave stands in the kitchen doorway with his back to Di. A pause

Ah, Dave, I don't know if I can do it in this position now.
Dave I love it when you talk dirty.
Di It's all right for men, you can do it up against the nearest wall.

In the Walshes' part, Ray finds a bottle, opens and smells it

Ray Whisky, no. (*He replaces it and smells another*)

Act II

Di You know wha', one of the first things we're goin' to do when we move in, if we move in? We're goin' to 'ave a downstairs toilet.
Dave Ray knows what he's doin', he said. It's just a matter of dottin' the t's and crossin' the i's.
Ray Gin, no. (*He replaces it and smells another*)
Di And when is he goin' to do all tha'?
Dave Tonight, he 'opes ... only he didn't bank on 'er upstairs spendin' all night in the Khazi.
Di We've got to get 'er out, Dave.
Dave Maybe we should send for a doctor or somethin'.
Di A psychiatrist ... says me peein' in the ice bucket.

They scream laughing

Hey, I'm like the bear on top of the Fox's Glacier Mint by here.

They both laugh helplessly. A beat as they pull themselves together

Dave Have you finished?
Di Yes. Get me some toilet paper, will you?
Dave Toilet paper? Oh, you 'aven't...
Di Wha'? Dave, get off ... wha' you take me for?
Dave Wha' do you want paper for, then?
Di Well... I do. We all do.

He gives her a strange look

Don't look like tha'. Men shake, women dab.
Dave The toilet paper's probably in the bathroom. (*He has an idea*) Will kitchen paper be all right?
Di Yeah, as long as it's not greaseproof.

They laugh again as Dave goes out to the kitchen

Ray Tha's the one... Vodka, no smell. Right, scam number one. (*He proceeds to empty the bottle up against the wall beside the cabinet*) Nice bit of damp by there.

Sheila is heard off in the Walshes' part

Sheila (*off*) Ray?

Sheila feels her way into the room

Ray?
Ray Wha'?
Sheila Barrie wants you.
Ray Wha' for?
Sheila He wants 'elp with the fuse.
Ray You're the clever one. Why don't *you* give 'im a 'and?
Sheila Well, 'e asked for *you*.
Ray You got to be jokin'. I don't want to be anywhere near 'im when 'e's by tha' fuse box.
Sheila Why?
Ray Cos if 'e's true to form 'e might blow the bloody thing up and me and 'im along with it.
Sheila You're a cheeky bugger you are, you didn't mind me 'elpin' 'im.

At this point Gayle feels her way back into the room and creeps between Sheila and Ray

(*After a slight pause*) You don't think 'e could blow it up, do you?
Ray With a bit a luck 'e will. And with the lights back on, and with the damage 'e's already done, we can drop the price down by another five grand.

Gayle hears this and freezes

Sheila Sshh. You don't know who's about. How's the survey goin'?
Ray Like clockwork.
Sheila Wha's 'e said 'bout it?
Ray I 'aven't shown it to 'im yet.
Sheila If that Barrie blows everythin' up we'll never 'ave the light back on, and 'ow's Martyn goin' to see the bloody survey, then?
Ray Good point. (*He calls as he feels his way off*) Barrie, I'm comin', butt. Don't touch nothin' till I get there.

Ray exits

Di (*calling*) Hurry up, Dave. I'm not very comfortable by 'ere.
Sheila (*calling towards the kitchen*) How are things in the kitchen, luv? Denise? Are you there? How you gettin' on?

Sheila disappears into the kitchen, leaving Gayle alone in the room for a moment

In despair, Gayle feels her way back out to the hallway

Act II

Martyn comes in from upstairs on the Gibbon side

Martyn Listen, I don't think I'm going to be able to get Gayle out of the bathroom ... are you all right down there?
Di Yeah, yeah, I'm fine.

An awkward pause

I bet you're wonderin' why I'm sittin' like this, 'in' you?
Martyn No, no, not at—well, yes, it did cross my mind, yes.
Di *(improvising madly)* It's yoga. I'm into yoga.
Martyn *(not at all sure)* Right. So you're in the lotus position under all that, then, are you?
Di Well, you could say tha'.

Dave comes in from the kitchen

Dave I couldn't find any kitchen roll... *(He sees Martyn)* Oohh ... you're down, then. *(To Di)* So you'll 'ave to make do with this. *(He holds some paper out to her)*
Di Wha' is it?
Dave Rice-paper. *(He throws it to her. To Martyn)* Everythin' all right now, is it?
Martyn No, not really.
Di *(taking it from him)* I can't use rice-paper.

Martyn looks at her

I needed somethin' to wipe my...
Dave Er ... wipe her nose.
Martyn Oh, allow me. *(He offers her his handkerchief)*

She hesitantly accepts

(To Dave) Listen, the problem I've got is Gayle. She's still in the bathroom. I think we're going to have to break the door down.
Dave *I* can kick tha' in for you.
Di No, you can't ... tha's goin' to be *our* door, remember.
Martyn I thought she was over it. She said she was. I'd never have let her come here if I thought for one minute... *(He has a horrible thought)* Ray wouldn't keep a razor in there, would he?
Dave I don't know.
Di Yeah, he does.
Martyn *(panicking)* Oh God.

Di But it's 'lectric.
Martyn (*very relieved*) Thank heavens for that.
Di Sheila uses an open one to shave 'er legs, mind.
Martyn Jesus.
Dave Wha's a matter?
Di I don't think she'd go and do something like that.
Martyn You don't know what she'd do when she's like this.
Dave Hey, keep calm now. We'll 'ave 'er out if it kills 'er...

Both Martyn and Di look at him

Well, you know wha' I mean.
Di (*to Dave; almost teasing*) Said the wrong thing by there, didn't you?

Ray comes in from outside on the Gibbon side

Ray Wha's the point in 'avin' a barbecue if you're goin' to spend all your time in the 'ouse.
Dave (*cracking his knuckles*) Ray, looks like we've got a bit of a problem 'ere.
Ray (*seeing Di*) Wha' you doin down there?
Dave Never mind 'er. It's 'is missis. She won't come out and he's asked me to kick the door in.
Ray Oh, I don't know 'bout tha'. Tha's a new door, tha' is. Cost a lot of money.
Martyn I've tried everything, but I don't understand it. Nothing works. I can usually reach her.
Ray Usually? You mean she's been like this before?
Martyn (*nodding*) You know she's a bit highly strung.
Dave (*to Ray*) Wha' did I tell you?
Martyn Maybe if someone else were to talk to her. A woman perhaps.

All three men look down at Di

Di Oh, don't all look at me, *I* don't know 'er.
Martyn Sometimes strangers are best.
Ray I'll get Sheila. They don't come stranger than 'er.

Ray laughs and goes out to the garden

Di gets up off the ice bucket and straightens her dress

Martyn (*pointing to the drinks bar*) Do you think Ray would mind if I helped myself to something?

Act II 55

Dave shakes his head

I wasn't going to drink tonight but I think I need one. (*He moves to the drinks bar*)
Dave (*almost whispering to Di*) How 'ave you managed?
Di I've dripped dry, haven't I?
Martyn Look, I haven't discussed it with Gayle yet, but I'm thinking of taking the house off the market.
Di (*slightly panicked*) No ... you can't do tha'. Dave, tell him ... 'e can't. Sheila'll be very disappointed.
Dave (*going over to Martyn at the bar*) Have you really thought 'bout this?
Martyn It's been a headache ever since we started. If you'd seen the surveyor's report——
Dave Seen it? I... I ... 'aven't, no. (*Slightly on the offensive*) Wha's the matter with it?
Martyn If it's anything to go by, it's amazing our house is still standing. I couldn't believe it, so I went and had my own done.
Dave (*alarmed*) What? What did it say?
Martyn (*lying*) Um... I haven't had it back yet. It'll probably say the same as Ray's. These things never differ *that* much, do they? Whoever would be interested in buying our house now would have problems raising a mortgage.
Dave Unless they paid cash.
Martyn Are *you* interested?
Dave No, I wasn't talking about me.
Martyn Where would *I* find a cash buyer?
Di You might if the price was right. (*She bends down to pick up the ice bucket*)
Martyn No, no... I couldn't in all conscience sell it ... not now.
Dave Not even to Ray?
Martyn Especially not to Ray. I like him, he's a good old sort and I couldn't do it to him.
Dave At the end of the day, you want to look after number one, mate.
Di Yeah.
Martyn That sounds strange coming from Ray's brother.
Dave It's a jungle out there ... anyway, same mother——
Dave ⎫
Di ⎭ (*together*) Different father.
Martyn He wouldn't want it now anyway. Not now that he's got his dream bungalow. (*He hands Dave and Di a drink*)

Di hands Martyn back his handkerchief

Sheila comes in from the garden, she has had a few drinks by this time and is carrying a half-drunk bottle of something. Ray follows her in

Sheila (*making a noise like a siren*) Make way... Sheila to the rescue. (*She laughs, hysterically*) All right, let the cat see the rabbit. Where is she?
Ray You know where she is, she's in the bathroom.
Sheila Don't you worry, Martyn, luv... *I'll* 'ave 'er out now, Mart'. She'll be in tha' garden drinkin' with us now before you got time to say, "Open to offers". (*She laughs again*)
Ray She's a bit worse for wear.
Sheila Come on, Di, come up with me. (*She dumps her bottle in the ice bucket—its contents splash everywhere. She insists*) Come on, come up. Ray, keep an eye on those beefburgers. Burn those buggers and we're in shit street.

Sheila goes off upstairs, followed by Di who hands the ice bucket to Dave as she goes

Dave looks, not sure what to do with it

Ray She'll be down now, Mart. Top-up anyone? (*He goes to the bar*)
Martyn Not for me.
Dave *I'll* 'ave another one. (*He drinks up. As he returns his glass to the bar he nods to Ray*)

Ray gets the message and speaks to Martyn

Ray Will you do us a favour, Mart? Check on those burgers for me, butt?

Martyn is happy to oblige

(*Calling after him*) Throw a bit more paraffin on, if you need to.

Martyn goes out to the garden, wiping his sweaty brow in his hanky as he goes

Dave (*after a slight pause*) He's swallowed tha' story 'bout you and the bungalow——
Ray Good.
Dave But you've got a problem. He's changed his mind 'bout sellin'.
Ray No 'e 'asn't.
Dave He told me. Tha' dodgy survey's back-firing on you.
Ray Every man's got 'is price and I'm goin' to end up 'aving tha' 'ouse for a song.
Dave He's ordered his own survey.
Ray I know.

Act II

Dave (*surprised*) Do you? How?
Ray (*tapping his nose*) Contacts.

On the Walshes' side, Gayle feels her way back into the room and sits nervously on the settee

Dave (*to Ray*) So wha' are you goin' to do now, then, eh? (*He answers himself*) Buy it quick before it comes back.
Ray It's already come back.
Dave (*a little confused*) Wha'?
Ray He don't know I *know* tha', mind. He thinks he's pulled a fast one, but I'm one step 'head of 'im.
Dave How *do* you know?
Ray (*tapping his nose*) Everythin's goin' like clockwork. All I got to do is get the money from you, sign on the dotted line and get 'im to agree to do the same tonight.
Dave I think tha' clock of yours is runnin' a bit fast. He doesn't want to sell the 'ouse to you. He likes you, he said. He's got a conscience 'bout it.
Ray You worry too much.
Dave I don't think I'm gettin' through to you, little brother, am I? It'll crack Di up if we don't get this 'ouse now. If you don't pull it off, apart from everything else I plan to do to you, I will not be givin' you tha' loan.
Ray (*after a slight pause*) Dave, see if you can work this one out now, right. If I fail tonight, will I still be needin' a loan?
Dave (*a slight pause*) All right, fair enough, fair enough.

Martyn comes into his living-room

Martyn Hallo? Anyone here?
Denise (*off*) Martyn?
Martyn Yes. Denise, is it?

Denise comes in from the kitchen. She's had more than a little to drink

Denise That's right.

Sheila comes out of the kitchen on the Walsh side

Sheila I'm 'ere as well.
Martyn Sheila. I'm sorry. I sent you upstairs, didn't I?
Sheila Don't worry 'bout it.
Martyn I'm still looking for Gayle. You haven't seen her?
Sheila *I* 'aven't seen any bugger since the lights went out.

Martyn She hasn't been in the kitchen with you, then?
Denise Definitely not. Would have known. I mean, I know it's dark, but you have a sense of who's in the room, don't you? If Gayle had been anywhere near us we'd have known.
Martyn (*feeling his way out of the room; calling*) Gayle? Gayle? Look, I know you're not talking to me, but... Just tell me you haven't done anything silly, that's all. Gayle?

Martyn feels his way out of the room and into the hallway

Sheila Silly? Wha' 'e mean by tha'?
Denise Personally I think she's in need of help.
Sheila Well, we're doin' wha' we can, 'in' we, Den'? Imagine wha' she'd 'ave been like if she didn't 'ave us 'ere to give a 'and.
Denise Meant in her private life. Reading between the lines, I don't think they get on very well, you know.
Sheila (*amazed*) Don't you? I thought they got on better than me and Ray, I did. Fancy a drink? (*She makes her way to the drinks cabinet*)
Dave (*to Ray on the Gibbon side*) You know, I can't work out 'ow you're so laid-back about it all.
Denise (*confidentially*) I came in earlier on and found her crying.
Sheila Gayle?
Dave You're so cocksure of everythin'.
Denise He tried to say it was the onions.
Ray Tha's because, unlike your botched buildin' society job, I've thought it all out.
Denise She tried to make light of it.
Ray Looked at it from all the angles.
Denise But she's in a terrible state.
Dave And Sheila's pretty cool 'bout it as well.
Denise And it's not just the stress of selling.
Dave How come she's not givin' you gyp?
Ray She trusts me, don't she.
Denise If you ask me, I think there's more going on here than meets the eye.
Sheila Is there? Like wha'?
Ray She knows I would never let 'er down.
Dave (*jokingly*) She don't know you very well, then.
Denise Well, if you want my professional opinion...
Ray Wha' you mean?
Denise *I* think he's seeing someone.
Sheila (*amazed*) He's carryin' on, you mean?

Gayle reacts

Act II 59

Dave Tha' fling you said you 'ad. I don't think Di would trust me if I'd been 'avin' it off with someone else.
Ray Sheila wouldn't trust *me* if I *told* 'er.
Denise Things are very tense between them.
Sheila I can't say I've noticed, Den'.
Dave So you 'aven't told 'er?
Ray Wha' you take me for?
Denise With all due respect, dear, you wouldn't.
Dave You said you didn't 'ave any secrets between you.
Denise I'm trained for that sort of thing.
Ray No, I didn't. I said *Sheila* doesn't 'ave any secrets from me.
Denise If he isn't having an affair I'll eat my hat.
Sheila (*very impressed*) It's marvellous 'ow you can tell like tha'.
Ray I didn't say nothin' 'bout me 'aving secrets from *'er*.
Sheila (*after a slight pause*) Wha' you make of my Ray?
Denise Sorry?
Ray (*lying*) Anyway, it was all a long time ago.
Sheila Do you think 'e might be buggerin' 'bout?
Denise (*can't imagine the thought*) Seeing someone else, you mean?
Ray It's all over now.
Denise (*dismissively*) Good heavens, no.
Sheila Hey... I didn't like the way you said tha', then.
Ray And a good thing too. It was a big mistake.
Sheila He's 'ad 'is chances, luv, let me tell you.
Denise I didn't mean to imply...
Dave Who was she? You never told me?
Sheila And so 'ave I too, mind.
Denise I'm sure.
Ray (*still lying*) You wouldn't know 'er. Wouldn't 'ave liked 'er either ... wasn't like Sheila at all.
Sheila So just get one thing straight now, right?
Ray A bit on the common side really.
Sheila We're not with each other 'cos we can't get no bugger else.
Denise Of course not.
Sheila I mean, I know Ray can be a bit on the common side.
Ray A bit of an old dog.
Sheila But I'm with 'im 'cos I *want* to be.
Denise Interesting.
Ray I know you won't say nothin'.
Sheila And 'e would never think of 'avin' an affair anyway.
Dave I wouldn't bank on it, bruv.
Ray I don't know wha' Sheila'd do if she found out.
Sheila He knows, I'd string 'im up by the bloody balls if 'e did.

Dave (*threateningly*) You want to make sure she don't, then, know wha' I mean? I think you want to get 'er down quick, or there'll be trouble, "Big time".
Sheila Here you are, Den'.

Sheila hands a drink to who she thinks is Denise but is in fact Gayle. Gayle drinks it and passes the empty glass to Denise

Suddenly, Martyn rushes in from the garden on the Gibbon side

Martyn (*out of breath and in a panic*) Quick. You've got to come quick!
Ray Don't tell me you've gone and burnt those bloody beefburgers?
Martyn No no. It's Gayle.
Ray The girls will 'ave 'er down now.
Martyn You don't understand.
Ray Have another drink with us by 'ere.
Martyn (*shouting*) She's on the roof. She's climbed out of the bathroom window and she's threatening to throw herself off the kitchen roof.

Ray and Dave look at each other before rushing off into the garden, followed hastily by Martyn

Ray (*off*) Bloody woman!
Sheila So you're some kind of marriage guidance councillor, then, are you?
Denise No, no ... doing a psychology course. Open University.

Denise and Sheila drink up... Denise looks confused when she realises there is no drink in the glass

Martyn (*off*) Hold on, Gayle, they're just getting a ladder.

Ray returns on the Gibbon side, followed quickly by Dave. They rush off into the passage

Sheila You reckon she knows 'bout this other woman, then, do you, Den'?
Denise She probably suspects something, but can't bring herself to confront it.
Sheila You're very good.
Denise (*flattered*) Well, I am top of my class.

Ray and Dave, carrying the ladders, rush off out into the garden

Sheila I was bloody awful in school, I was. Never took any notice, see. Sorry now, mind, but tha's life, innit?

Act II

Martyn comes into the living-room on the Walsh side

Martyn Hallo?
Sheila Yes, we're still 'ere, Mart'.
Martyn God, this is silly now. She's hiding from me.
Denise Interesting. Why do you think she'd be doing that?
Martyn (*mocking her*) Well, perhaps *you'd* like to tell *me*.
Denise Did you hear that, Sheila?
Sheila Wha'?
Denise Martyn's tone. It's developing an edge.
Martyn (*impatiently*) No, it's not! I'm just worried about Gayle, that's all. You don't know what she's like.
Denise Why don't you tell us.
Martyn She's avoiding me.
Sheila Don't be soft, it's dark, mun.
Martyn She is, I know she is … it's because of what I said.
Sheila (*a little shocked*) You didn't tell 'er about your affair, did you, Mart'?
Martyn Affair? What affair? I'm not having an affair.
Denise (*to Sheila*) I told you that in confidence.
Martyn Excuse me. (*Determinedly*) I am not having an affair. What the hell made you think that?
Denise (*to Sheila*) Golden rule, never involve yourself in other people's business.
Martyn She's not talking to me because of what I said to *you*, Sheila.
Sheila Me?
Martyn Yes. (*He rambles*) I said some things I shouldn't have to someone I shouldn't have said them to. I said them to *Gayle*… I said she was neurotic.
Denise I think you probably did the right thing by saying what you did, Martyn.
Martyn You do?
Denise It's very important you be honest with her.
Martyn Yes, it is, isn't it?
Denise If she were here now I'd probably say exactly the same thing myself.
Sheila Yeah, and I would.

Suddenly the Lights come back on and Ray and Barrie shout with success from offstage. Sheila and Denise immediately see that they are sitting either side of Gayle on the sofa. They take one look at each other, then at Martyn

Sheila and Denise run out of the room

Martyn and Gayle are left alone together. A pause. Martyn tries to laugh but can't quite pull it off

Martyn Let me explain.

Gayle chases Martyn off into the hallway

(*Off*) You have to admit, I do have to keep an eye on you.

Gayle (*off; shouting*) After what that Denise said about *you*, it's you who needs to be watched.

There is no-one in either room at this point. Suddenly voices are heard shouting off in Ray's garden. The following sequence between Ray and Martyn is recorded

Ray (*off*) Careful, now, Gayle ... hold the ladder steady. (*Shouting*) Both 'ands, both 'ands.

Martyn (*off*) Hold on tight and take your time, Gayle.

Ray (*off*) Yes, go on ... grab the drainpipe if it 'elps.

Martyn (*off*) That's good, you're doing well, Gayle. Now the other foot.

Ray (*off; shouting*) Don't look down! God, she nearly went then.

Martyn (*off*) Just keep putting one foot behind the other.

Ray (*off*) That's it, you've got it now, leave the drainpipe, go. No, leave it go. If you'll just leave it go ... oh God!

Martyn (*off*) Don't worry, I'll pay for it. Down you come. I've got you, Gayle, I've got you.

There is one almighty crash from the garden

End of recorded dialogue

Gayle chases Martyn back into the Walsh living-room around the sofa

You didn't believe all that about an affair, did you?

She gives him a look

She's a quack. She doesn't know what the hell she's talking about.

Gayle (*picking up a cushion from the sofa*) She seems to have done a pretty good job of diagnosing my neurosis. (*She is ready to hit him with the cushion*)

Martyn crouches down UL *of the sofa*

Martyn (*insisting*) Now, Gayle, I am not having an affair. You've got to believe me!

Act II

Gayle (*after a slight pause, becoming upset*) I suppose I do let things get to me. Oh Martyn.

They embrace

How am I going to get through the rest of tonight?
Martyn It's OK, sweetheart, we've had a few set-backs, that's all ... but the lights are on now. No reason why we can't pick up from where we left off.
Gayle But what about that survey? He's got it with him. That Ray. He's going to show it to you. It's not good news, Martyn, it pulls the place to pieces. It says something about subsidence and underpinning. It's ten thousand pounds worth of work.
Martyn Well, whatever it is, I don't want you worrying about it. Now you sit there and you be strong. Let me get you a drink. (*He goes to the drinks cabinet to pour two glasses*) What the hell is the matter with the wall? (*He touches it*) It's all wet.
Gayle (*panicking*) It's not running down from the ceiling, is it?
Martyn No, it's only half way up. That's odd.
Gayle I told you something's afoot.
Martyn Now don't start that again.

Denise pops out of the kitchen

Denise Coo-ee. Just thought I'd let you know. Slight problem.

Gayle looks petrified at her

I was going to do something really exciting with tinned tomatoes. I opened them in the dark, only to realize it's tins of rice pudding.

Denise laughs as she pops back into the kitchen

Gayle looks at Martyn, who makes a fist and gestures with his arm for her to strengthen her resolve

Ray and Dave come back into the living-room from the garden on the Gibbon side

Gayle Something odd happened in the dark. That Sheila and Ray were talking. They didn't know I was in the room, Martyn. She asked if things were going well. Yes, he said ... like clockwork. They were talking about the survey. Something isn't right. They're definitely up to something.

Sheila comes in from upstairs on the Gibbon side

Sheila Marvellous, innit. Me an' Di been coaxin' our guts out tryin' to get 'er to open tha' door, an' it turns out she's not even in the bloody bathroom.
Gayle And *then* there's the Lovejoys'.
Sheila *I* think you'd better get out there, Ray, and start shiftin' things.
Dave I do as well.
Ray You've got to give 'em time to make their move, mun.
Sheila (*sharply*) Ray!

Ray immediately goes off into the garden

Gayle There's more to *them* than meets the eye.
Sheila Di will be down now. She's puttin' on a different dress ... said tha' one made 'er feel silly.
Gayle What are we going to do?
Sheila (*going to the bar*) Don't know about you, Dave, but I fancy a drink.
Martyn There's only one thing we can do ... get our own survey done.
Sheila Any more ice here, looks like this lot's melted.
Dave Oh, hell...
Sheila What?

Dave is about to say something, but stops

Dave Nothin'.
Martyn (*thinking hard*) We mustn't show we suspect anything.
Gayle No.
Sheila (*pouring a drink*) What are you having?
Dave I got a beer, I have.
Sheila (*holding the glass of wine*) Oh, this is bloody warm. Never mind. (*She drinks it down in one and pours herself another before returning the bottle to the ice bucket*)
Martyn (*still trying to work out the best way forward*) We carry on acting as normal.
Gayle I'm not going to let them get away with anything, Martyn.
Martyn No, but it won't do any harm to let them *think* they're getting away with something.

Di comes in from upstairs on the Gibbon side, wearing a different dress... It's not really an improvement

Dave And you said the other one made you look silly.
Di Wha's the matter with it?
Sheila Nothin', luv. I wore tha' to my friends weddin'. (*She takes the bottle from the ice bucket and pours a drink*) You are, 'ave this.

Act II

Martyn Sooner or later Ray's bound to make his move.
Di No, ta.
Sheila (*insisting*) 'Ave it, mun. I've poured it now.
Di I don't want it, all right?.
Sheila Oh, please your bloody self, then. (*She drinks it*)

Di looks at Dave, who shrugs his shoulders

Sheila and Ray go out into the garden

Martyn And in the meantime, we start making ours. (*He picks up the phone book, looks for a number and dials*)
Di Oh Dave, I don't know about you, but I'm starvin'.
Dave Hey, you know what *I* fancy?
Di Yeah, I bet it's not a burger.

They look at each other, before he starts to chase her around the room

Come on, come and get it.

Di and Dave laugh as the disappear off upstairs

Martyn (*to Gayle*) Answering machine. (*Into the phone*) Yes, it's Martyn Walsh here on eight four five two six seven. I'd like to make an appointment to have a survey done on my home, please.

At this point Ray comes into the room, he senses what's going on and backs out, but stays to listen just outside the door

It is rather urgent, so if you could call me back first thing on Monday morning I'd be very grateful. Thank you very much. (*He hangs up*) Yes!

Ray comes in from the hall

Ray Right. Do you want the good news or the bad news? Well, the bad news is you've got a crack in your stairs ... and the good news is, I've just talked Barrie out of repairin' it.
Martyn Excellent.
Ray I didn't 'ave much luck with the porch door, though. He sent me in to ask if you got any putty.

Martyn and Gayle look at each other. Gayle is very uptight and cannot take much more. She has made up her mind to sort Barrie out herself

Gayle I'm sorry... I'm sorry.

Gayle leaves the room screaming

(*Off*) Barrie!
Martyn She's not taking things very well.
Ray Understandable, given the night she's 'ad.
Martyn Have a drink, shall we?
Ray Why not.

Martyn makes to do it

No, you stay there, I'll make 'em now... What's your poison? (*He goes over to the cabinet*)
Martyn Vodka, please.
Ray Due due... Wha's this, you got a bit of damp comin' in by 'ere.
Martyn I don't think so.
Ray Yes, it's soaking with you. Mind you, it mentioned it in the survey.
Martyn (*suspiciously*) Did it. (*Realizing how it sounded, he repeats himself, this time sounding much more concerned*) I mean, did it?
Ray There's no easy way of tellin' you this... perhaps you'd better sit down and read it for yourself. (*He takes out a large brown envelope from his pocket and hands it to Martyn*) I've underlined all the, er, major defects.

A pause as Martyn scans the document

Pages two and three.

Martyn turns to the pages and continues to read on

I got to tell you, mind, it puts a 'hole new light on the situation. (*To take up the pause, he wonders around the room a little, whistling*)

Sheila comes in from the kitchen, loudly

Sheila I was just saying——

Unseen by Martyn, Ray waves his hand for her to go away

Sheila understands immediately and does an about turn, finishing her line as she goes back into the kitchen

—now...

Act II

Eventually Martyn sighs, heavily

Ray So Martyn, wha' do you think?
Martyn (*testing the water*) I don't suppose you want to buy the house now.
Ray Oh, I wouldn't say tha'. Perhaps if we can make some sort of a deal?
Martyn (*after a slight pause*) How much exactly are we talking about?
Ray Twelve grand?

Martyn shakes his head as he has an intake of breath through his teeth

But I think I can get it done for ten.
Martyn (*after a slight pause*) Patterson Associates. Do you know I don't think I've heard of these people. Do you mind if I keep this?
Ray No, no ... not at all. (*He takes the survey back from him*) I'll 'ave to get you a copy, though, I need this one for now. (*He puts it back in his pocket, quickly*) Drink?
Martyn No, thanks. You can pour yourself one, though. There's no way I can drop ten grand.
Ray (*cautiously*) Think now wha' you're sayin' now, Mart'. Per'aps wha' you mean is, you don't *want* to drop ten grand.
Martyn Of course I don't *want* to.
Ray But wha' you've got to ask yourself, see, is, 'ow keen are you *and* Gayle to buy the Lovejoys', and 'ow much are you prepared to sell this 'ouse to me for.
Gayle (*off; desperately*) Martyn!
Martyn Excuse me a minute.
Gayle (*off; even more desperately*) Martyn!!

Martyn goes off to see Gayle

As soon as he's left the room, Ray presses re-dial on the phone and leaves another message

Ray (*in his best Martyn voice*) Oh, hallo, this is Martyn Walsh here again, I called two minutes ago. I'm very sorry, I've checked my diary and I can't do next Monday. I'll call back again, thank you. (*He hangs up*)

Gayle comes in, pushing Barrie in front of her

Gayle I don't care... I don't care! Please, listen to me. I don't *want* my gas meter moved.
Barrie I didn't mean tonight. I'd be quite happy to come back tomorrow and do it for you then.

Denise comes out of the kitchen

Denise Thought I heard his master's voice. Everything all right?
Barrie Yes.
Gayle No!
Denise (*thrilled*) You wouldn't believe what I've just managed to do with a tin of corned beef and half a dozen eggs.
Gayle (*outraged*) I can't give you corned beef and eggs ... not after planning *épinards à la niçoise*.

Sheila comes out of the kitchen with a cigarette in one hand and an empty egg carton in the other

Sheila Hey Den', know those eggs you used?

Denise nods

Look at the date on tha'. (*She hands her the carton*)

Gayle is just about to crumple, but again she looks at Martyn who gestures for her to stay strong. She rallies

Gayle (*annoyed, frustrated, but with resolve*) I'm going to cook a meal tonight if it's the last thing I do.

Gayle goes into the kitchen, slamming the door behind her

Sheila I'm no' bein' funny, but in *tha'* mood it probably will be.
Martyn (*very confident*) She'll be all right. (*But he's not sure*)
Sheila Thank God I spotted the date ... we'd 'ave all been down with bloody salmonella ... speaking of which. It's all right to use the bathroom now, Mart', is it?
Martyn Yes.
Barrie Well, no...
Ray He's still got the floor up.
Sheila Well, I've got to go, 'aven't I, Ray? I got a problem, see, can't 'old on to it for long.
Barrie Right, I'll sort that out for you in a jiffy.
Martyn (*sharply*) No! No, stay here, stay here and help yourself to a drink.

A beat

Ray Come on, darlin'... I'll take you up.

Act II   69

Ray and Sheila go upstairs

Martyn (*calling after Ray*) Give me a shout when you've finished ... you can help me to put the floor back.
Barrie It's nothing for me to——
Martyn No, it's fine ... no, honestly.
Barrie (*after a slight pause*) You did say I could help myself?

Martyn gestures for him to carry on

What would you like, Denise?
Denise Anything ... as long as it's large.
Barrie And you?
Martyn No, not at the moment.

Barrie moves to the drinks cabinet

Barrie I say. I say ... what's this damp patch here? (*He pours Denise a drink*)
Martyn It's nothing.
Barrie It doesn't look like nothing to me. That's bad, that. It's rising too, by the look of it.
Martyn It wasn't there this morning.
Barrie It's on the gallop, then. You ought to get someone to have a look at it.
Martyn Yes, I will.
Barrie I could look at it for you if——
Martyn No.
Barrie It's not a big job. (*He hands Denise her drink*)
Martyn No.
Barrie It's only a question of knocking the plaster off and——
Martyn No.
Barrie Treating it with...

There is a long pause

No?

Martyn shakes his head

Denise Hope Ray hasn't spotted it. It could put him off. If he were to back out now——
Barrie The whole chain would collapse.
Denise And we don't want that ... do we?

Barrie Well, we won't be pointing it out to him, will we, Denise?

Ray calls from upstairs. This is pre-recorded

Ray (*off*) Oi, Martyn! Martyn.
Martyn Excuse me a minute. Oh, and Barrie ... you won't touch anything, will you?

Martyn calls to Ray as he goes off

What do you want, Ray?
Ray (*off*) Don't panic now, right? But 'ave a guess wha' tha' Barrie 'as done with your bedroom door.

Barrie and Denise look at each other

Barrie Well, I had to stand on something.
Denise (*smiling*) Some people are never grateful.

He smiles wickedly back

Well, this is all very encouraging, don't you think?

Sheila and Ray come in from the garden on the Gibbon side

Ray Believe me, Sheil', I got 'em eatin' out of my 'and.
Denise Can't see that Ray and Sheila going through with anything now, can you?
Ray By the time I've finished here tonight, they'll be begging me to take it off 'em.
Barrie We're not out of the woods yet, though ... as things stand, we'll still have to go through with the sale of our house.
Ray Where's Dave?
Sheila Upstairs with Di.
Ray (*calling upstairs*) Dave?

Ray goes upstairs

Denise Not when they back down and the chain collapses. When that happens that'll be the end of it.
Sheila Where are you going? You can't disturb 'em. Ray!
Denise Now all we have to do now is sait back and wait for Ray to pull out. Oh, I can't tell you what a weight it is off my mind. Don't think I could stand going through it all again.

Act II

Barrie Well, let's drink to the hope of not having to.

They raise their glasses and drink

Sheila looks into the ice bucket

Sheila Ice.

Sheila goes out to the kitchen

Denise Looks like you won't have to be selling the *Big Issue* after all, then, Barrie.

They both laugh

Ray comes in from upstairs on the Walsh side

Ray I wish *I* 'ad somethin' to laugh about.
Denise Are you *very* disappointed? You must be. Still, probably for the best. There'll be other houses I'm sure.
Ray Wha' you talkin' 'bout? We 'aven't lost it yet.
Denise Oh ... but with all the faults ... the survey ... surely you're not still going through with the purchase?
Ray If I can get 'em to drop ten grand I will.
Barrie (*beginning to panic*) No, you mustn't.
Ray Wha'?
Barrie You can't go ahead with it now.
Ray I can't?
Barrie Not in the light of everything.
Ray Why not?
Barrie (*he struggles to tell him and fails*) Denise?
Denise (*after a pause*) Well, now we'll *have* to put him in the picture, won't we? (*She pauses slightly*) The thing is ... we seem to have found ourselves... Can I speak to you in absolute confidence?
Ray Goes without sayin'.
Denise (*after a slight pause*) Well, the fact of the matter is ... how shall I put this...
Barrie We've got a bit of a problem.
Denise The house we want to buy...
Barrie Isn't for sale anymore.
Denise They took it off the market yesterday.
Barrie That was very disappointing for us...
Denise But to make matters worse...

Barrie We signed and exchanged to sell to...
Denise Martyn and Gayle...
Barrie The day before. We couldn't *really* see a way out...
Denise Until you said about the survey...
Barrie And pointed out what was wrong with the place.
Denise If *you* didn't go ahead with the purchase...
Barrie *We* wouldn't be forced to sell our house...
Denise And rent something...
Barrie So everything would work out fine, but on the other hand...
Denise If you *did* insist on going through with it...
Barrie Well...
Denise }
Barrie } (*together*) You can see our problem, can't you?

There is a pause

On the Gibbons' side, Sheila comes back in from the kitchen empty-handed

Ray So let me get this straight now. You don't want me to buy this 'ouse, 'cos you've technically sold yours and 'aven't got nowhere to live.
Denise Well, wouldn't have put it *exactly* like that...
Barrie But in a nutshell...
Denise }
Barrie } (*together*) Yes.

A slight pause

Ray The thing is, see, Sheila got 'er 'eart set on this place. We've bought a lot of things to go in here already, like.
Denise Well, we wouldn't want you to be out of pocket, of course...
Barrie So what do you think? Can we come to some sort of arrangement?
Ray Financial, you mean?
Barrie I haven't got to tell you how important it is to us.
Ray No, I can see tha'.

Barrie and Denise look at each other

The thing is, you're askin' a 'ell of a lot.
Barrie We do realize.
Denise And as I say, we are prepared to compensate you.
Ray How much?
Barrie Name a price.
Ray Well, it's not goin' to be cheap I can tell you tha'.

Act II

Denise How much do you want?
Ray Ten grand.
Barrie Ten grand? That's ridiculous.
Ray All right, nine, then.
Denise One thousand pounds.
Ray Tha' wouldn't even pay my costs.
Barrie Two.
Ray Seven.
Denise Two.
Ray Wha' 'bout Sheila?
Denise Three.
Ray Five.
Barrie Three.
Ray Four.
Barrie Three.
Ray Four and a 'alf.
Barrie Three.
Denise Three thousand to stay where you are, that can't be bad.
Ray (*after a slight pause*) I'll think 'bout it.
Barrie What's there to think about?
Ray Well, I've still got every confidence tha' Martyn will come down, see. Three thousand pounds might sound like a lot of money, but ten thousand is even more.

Barrie and Denise look at each other, defeated

I'll tell you wha'. I'll 'ave a chat to Sheila, and I'll see wha' I can sort out.
Barrie You won't say anything to, er ... Martyn and Gayle, will you? I can trust you on that?
Ray Barrie, my old cock ... my lips are sealed.
Denise It's just that ... we're in a pretty precarious situation.
Ray Not puttin' too fine a point on it, you're in bloody shit street, luv'.

Ray laughs as he leaves

Barrie and Denise look at each other

Barrie I don't know about you...
Denise But I think we might have just made one huge mistake.
Barrie (*after a slight pause*) Let's go home?
Denise (*shaking her head*) I haven't given up yet. Come on.
Barrie Where are you going?
Denise We don't know *what* he might be saying to him. We shouldn't leave them alone together.

Denise and Barrie go off upstairs

Our focus turns to the Gibbon room

Sheila (*shouting from the bar, really impatiently*) Ray! Are you 'aving a bloody threesome up there or wha'?

Sheila goes off upstairs as Martyn and Gayle sheepishly appear from the garden. He has his arm around her and she looks extremely distraught. They drop the pretence, though, as soon as they realize there is no-one in the room

Martyn Right, so far so good.
Gayle Where *is* everyone?

Martyn shrugs

What are we going to do now?
Martyn Don't worry, it'll be fine. They won't let us go home before they make their move.
Gayle Ray hasn't mentioned the house once, you said?
Martyn He gave me some cock and bull story about a bungalow.
Gayle But what if it's true?
Martyn He wants our house and we want him to have it, Gayle. It's just a question of when Ray makes his move.
Gayle Time's running out. One of us will have to do something soon.

Sheila comes back in from upstairs

Sheila Oh... (*She tries to laugh on seeing Martyn and Gayle*) There you are. Everythin' all right?

They each smile and almost nod

You goin' to 'ave a drink?
Martyn Er, no ... better not.
Sheila Go on, you can 'ave a little one.
Martyn We'll be going soon.

Gayle looks at him

Sheila Wha'?
Martyn Gayle isn't feeling up to it.

Act II

Sheila (*slightly panicked*) Oh ... you can't go, Gayle, not yet.
Martyn And we've got a big day tomorrow what with the, er...
Gayle Wedding...
Martyn And everything.
Gayle But I couldn't leave without apologising first. I know I've made a fool of myself.
Martyn (*encouragingly*) No, you haven't.
Sheila Well, she 'as, but it's only in front of us, innit? I'll tell Ray now. (*She goes to the passage and calls*) Ray? (*She waits for a reply*) Ray! (*She calls again*) They're goin' bloody 'ome!
Ray (*off*) I'll be down now.
Sheila (*coming back into the room*) I thought tha' would shift 'im. You 'aven't 'ad nothin' to eat.
Gayle We're not hungry ... are we, Martyn?
Martyn No, we've lost our appetites.

Ray comes in from upstairs, followed by Dave and Di

Ray Wha's the problem?
Sheila They're goin' 'ome.
Martyn Yes, thanks for a lovely evening ... well, you know what I mean.

A slight pause

Right, then, Gayle. Off we go.

Sheila gives Ray a worried look. Martyn and Gayle quickly glance at each other

Ray (*after a pause*) Right, I'll show you to the door, then.

Martyn and Gayle walk hesitantly towards the door. They are near the hallway when Martyn gives in

Martyn Well, perhaps we could stay for just one more ... what do you think, Gayle?
Gayle (*reluctantly*) Just the one, then.

Ray breathes a sigh of relief and thinks he's got them now more or less where he wants them and goes confidently on with his scam

Sheila I'll get 'em. (*She goes to the bar and pours drinks for everyone*)
Gayle Nothing alcoholic for me.

Ray Have somethin' tidy, mun.
Sheila It's sorted.
Gayle I shouldn't have come really.
Martyn Her nerves are in a terrible state... (*To Gayle*) Still, you'll feel a lot better now we're taking the house off the market.
Sheila (*after a slight pause*) Ray?
Ray Think about wha' you're sayin' now, Mart'. Now Gayle, you might be feeling a bit bad now, but what are you going to be like when things start happening?
Gayle What things?
Ray I wouldn't mind bettin' you've got two inch cracks in your walls already.
Gayle We haven't seen any.
Ray Tha's because it's be'ind the wallpaper, innit. The trouble with subsidence, see, is it's a crafty little bugger. One morning you'll wake up and your telly's on the other side of the room.
Martyn I'm sure it hasn't come to that.
Ray Wha 'bout tha' damp patch I found in your 'ouse last week? It might not be there now, but after a couple of weeks, months, years, well, your whole 'ouse could fall down.
Gayle Oh God, Martyn ... what are we going to do?
Ray Piece of advice, get rid of it as quick as you can.
Martyn Well, it's easy to say that.
Ray There's bound to be somebody out there who would jump at a quick sale for cash.
Martyn True, but buyers don't grow on trees.
Ray Ay. Shame I put tha' offer in for the bungalow this morning. Don't get me wrong, it's a smashin' little place, innit, Sheil'?

She nods

But the truth is, she's 'ad 'er 'eart set on your 'ouse from the start.
Martyn (*keenly*) You mean, if you hadn't made an offer on the bungalow, you'd still be interested in our house?
Ray For thirty-five grand, ay.
Martyn Yes, but because of the survey you'd have difficulties raising a mortgage.
Ray (*realizing*) I 'aven't told you. I'm not having one. Dave's sortin' me out.
Dave I am, yeah.
Martyn (*tentatively*) Well, what about it, then? Do you fancy backing out of the bungalow?
Ray Well, it's not up to me, though, is it? Sheila? What do *you* think?
Sheila Well, to be 'onest, I don't mind wha' one I have really ... but if we'd be doin' you a favour like by 'avin' yours, well...

Act II

Ray (*after a slight pause*) Have we got a deal?
Martyn (*smiling triumphantly*) Looks like you've sold your 'ouse, Ray.

Everyone including Dave and Di scream with excitement

Ray No backin' out now, mind. Witnesses 'ere and everythin'. (*He laughs*)
Martyn Just don't come back to us if a wall falls down. (*He laughs*)
Ray I'll give you a ring tomorrow. Make arrangements to meet the solicitor on Monday.
Sheila Well, cheers, everybody.

They all drink a toast. Martyn and Gayle drink it down in one. A slight pause

Gayle Ready, then, Martyn?
Sheila You 'aven't got to go now, mind.
Gayle I have to take medication at ten.
Sheila Well, you shouldn't take tablets on an empty stomach. Have somethin' to eat before you go.
Martyn No, really.
Sheila Take a beefburger with you, then. (*She remembers*) Beefburger. Has anybody bothered to look at the bloody beefburgers...

Sheila runs out into the garden

A slight pause

Martyn Well, good night all.

Dave and Di shout good night as they smile and wave as Ray takes Martyn and Gayle out to the front door

Dave hands Di a drink

Ray (*to Martyn and Gayle*) Bit of advice now. Try not to look at it like you've lost ten grand. Think 'ow lucky you are you've found some bugger to take it off your 'ands.

Martyn and Gayle are gone

A slight pause

Dave Well ... he did it. (*Excitedly*) Just think, two weeks and we'll be in this place. (*He goes to Di and hugs her from behind, still with the drink in his hand*) Didn't I promise I'd buy you a nice 'ouse?

Di Yeah ... 'course I didn't know I'd 'ave to wait four years to get it.
Dave It's worth it, though, innit? At least I've got the money now to spoil you rotten.
Di You spoil me anyway.
Dave And don't you forget it. Fancy goin' back upstairs?
Di And 'ave Ray come bargin' in again? No. We'll 'ave to wait till bed time.
Dave Tha' could be past midnight.
Di Yeah, it could, yeah ... anyhow, we still got some serious drinkin' to do. (*She finishes her drink*) And we 'aven't eaten yet.
Dave There's nothin' stoppin' us nippin' up now. We can come back down for a drink and somethin' to eat.
Di (*shaking her head*) By the time I've finished with you you'll be fit for nothin', right? (*She kisses him*)
Dave (*after a slight pause*) Can I ask you somethin'?

She nods

Don't take this the wrong way now...

A slight pause

Well, it's somethin' tha' Martyn said earlier. (*He pauses slightly*) When I was inside... 'Ow did you manage?

She looks a little puzzled

Well, four years is a long time.
Di It was a long for you and all...
Dave He said, tha' Martyn, tha' he didn't think Gayle would wait for *him*.
Di Well, I waited for *you*.
Dave So tell me 'ow you managed, then.
Di (*after a slight pause*) I'll do a deal with you, I'll tell you how I managed if you'll tell me how *you* did.
Dave (*after a beat*) Fair enough, we'll knock it on the 'ead.

Sheila comes in from the garden, carrying a stack of black beefburgers

Sheila *Somebody's* goin' to get knocked on the 'ead. Look at the bloody state on these? (*She holds out the plate*)
Di Chuck 'em out, let's 'ave a drink.
Sheila (*she gets herself a drink*) Where's the piss'ead?
Di Oh, don't call 'im tha'. He did all right for us tonight.
Sheila Yeah, 'e did, didn't 'e? For a minute though I thought 'e'd buggered it all up.

Act II   79

Ray comes in from the passage

Ray (*smug with confidence*) Didn't I tell you it would all work out?
Sheila Never doubted you for a minute, sweet'eart.
Ray I reckon I deserve a drink.
Sheila Comin' up.
Ray This is my lucky day, this is. Not only 'ave I just made ten grand, I've earned myself a nice little bonus as well.

All three move closer and listen to what Ray has to say

   For a small fee I've agreed not to buy the Walshes'.
Sheila (*stunned*) Wha'?
Di If you're not buying their house, who is?
Ray You are!
Di I don't want their house.
Ray Tha's all right, 'cos you're not 'avin' it.
Sheila You've confused me now, Ray.
Dave I'm not sure *I'm* with you either.
Ray (*to Dave and Di*) Listen, you're goin' to buy the Walshes' and sell it straight to me ... for a quid.
Sheila Why can't *we* buy it?
Ray 'Cos I've accepted a three thousand... (*He corrects himself immediately*) I've accepted a thousand pounds—one thousand pounds from the Lovejoys not to.
Di Why would they pay you to do that?
Ray Long story.
Dave Hang on a minute... 'ang on. If you've made a quick thousand by here...
Ray Don't worry, I'll split it with you. You shall 'ave five hundred pounds in your 'and as soon as she's given it to me.
Dave That's all right, then. Just as long as you're not trying to pull a fast one?
Ray Would I do tha' to you? I thought you knew me better than tha'. (*He claps his hands*) Right! See to all the paperwork on Monday now ... and the rest is plain sailin'.
Dave Good job you're 'avin' the money off me. You'd never 'ave pulled this off with a mortgage.
Ray Yeah ... we're really lucky there. Right, then, you lot. (*He claps his hands*) Let's go out to this barbie!

They all laugh and chant, "let's all have a barbie", etc. As he makes his way to the back door, Ray spots the plate of burnt beefburgers

   Hey, wha' are those?

Sheila (*winking at the others*) Chocolate biscuits... 'Ave one.

Ray helps himself, taking a huge bite... But he immediately spits it out

Sheila laughs hysterically as Ray chases her out into the garden

Dave and Di are left alone. They become aware of the moment and both know what they'd like to do to each other. Then Di looks towards the kitchen door, then back at Dave. They smile at each other. Slowly Di walks to the bar and puts down her glass. She turns to him. A slight pause before she seductively walks to the passage door. She pauses and looks back at him. He, equally slowly, goes to the bar and places his glass. He looks game, then teases her by feigning a yawn

Dave Na... (*He heads for the garden, stopping briefly to look back over his shoulder at Di*)
Di Get your arse up these stairs, now!

Dave chases Di off

For a moment there is no-one in either room. We then move back to the previous Friday at the Walshes'

Gayle, uptight and on the brink of a breakdown, comes out of her kitchen

She closes the door immediately behind her, standing hard against it. She is in such a state. Eventually she walks across the room and almost collapses on the sofa

We hear Ray off

Ray (*off*) Hang on a minute, I'll ask 'er now.

Ray comes into the room

Gayle. Barrie wants to know if you'd like the two bedrooms knocked into one? (*He laughs*)

Gayle starts to cry like a baby at the news. Ray comforts her

I was only jokin', mun. Martyn and Barrie are puttin' everythin' back as they found it.

This doesn't make her feel any better. A slight pause

Act II

Have you got a 'anky?

She is still too upset to answer

(*Attempting to change the subject*) How are things goin' in the kitchen?

Gayle begins to wail now

(*Going to the cabinet*) I'll make you a drink. Wha' you fancy... (*He looks at the various bottles*) Tia Maria, tha's lovely, innit? (*He pours her a large drink*)

Gayle (*still very emotional*) I still can't believe what's happened.
Ray You've got to calm down... (*He hands her the drink*) Get tha' down your neck.
Gayle (*drinking*) Nothing's gone right. Even the meal is a disaster.
Ray I take it we're not eatin', then?
Gayle I defy anyone to make a meal out of what's out there.
Ray Don't worry 'bout it, mun. You do get too uptight, tha's your trouble.
Gayle I know... I know ... my nerves are dreadful, I couldn't even open a Fray Bentos pie. If only I'd done a joint.
Ray (*after a slight pause*) Well, maybe I can 'elp you out by there.
Gayle Could you? If you did, I might just be able to save the day.
Ray You sit there and relax now, think positive.
Gayle Yes.
Ray There you are. (*He takes out a spliff and hands it to her*)
Gayle Oh, I need this.

Ray spots the lighter on the coffee table and lights it for her. Gayle drags long and hard. Exhaling, she looks at the cigarette between her fingers, realizing it's an odd taste but decides not to question it

Ray How you feelin' now? Any better?
Gayle (*after taking another drag*) Funnily enough, yes.
Ray Oh, it's great, innit? Nothin' fazes me now.
Gayle It must be marvellous to be like that.
Ray You'll get like it yourself one day.
Gayle Wouldn't it be wonderful? (*She takes another drag*)
Ray Honest, you'll wake up and everythin' won't seem so bad.
Gayle God, I'm hot. Is it hot or is it me?
Ray No, I'm all right.
Gayle Then it's me... I'm cooking.
Ray No, you're not ... you can't, there's bugger all there, that's why you're depressed, luv. (*He gives a little laugh*)

Suddenly Gayle gets the joke and laughs too. It develops into something hysterical. Eventually she manages to pull herself together

Gayle Oh Ray ... you've been here for hours. (*She laughs again*) People must be starving ... perhaps I should cook *something*.
Ray Well, only if you really want to.
Gayle Oh, I want to... (*She mocks his accent*) I wunt to. (*She laughs again, then takes another drag*) Do you think you could go and get it, then?
Ray Wha'?
Gayle I don't mind really, lamb would be nice.
Ray Sorry, but you've lost me now.
Gayle You said you could get a leg of lamb.
Ray (*really surprised*) I did?
Gayle Well, you said you could help me out. Pork will be fine, if it's easier.
Ray (*taking the spliff from her and dragging on it*) Where the 'ell am I goin' to get a piece of pork from at this time of night?
Gayle I don't know. (*She laughs hysterically, then says her next line in a thick Scottish accent*) Oh, I hope you're not going to let me down, Ray. (*She laughs even more*)
Ray I don't know where the 'ell you think I'm going to get a joint of... (*He looks down at the joint he has in his hands, realizes her mistake and mouths "oh fuck!" He realizes what's happened and starts to laugh*)

Gayle joins in, not sure what she's laughing at, so she asks him

Gayle What are you laughing at?
Ray (*still laughing*) When you said you needed a joint... (*Through his laughter he manages to squeeze out the line*) I thought you meant a spliff.

Gayle is laughing hysterically by now

Gayle (*still laughing*) What's a spliff? (*She takes the spliff back*)
Ray It's drugs, innit.
Gayle (*almost outraged*) I'm smoking drugs?

Ray is laughing too much to answer, but he nods

  (*After a beat*) Oh, fuck it. (*She takes another drag*)

This sends them both into more hysterics. Eventually they calm down and are able to speak

Ray Oh, this is one 'ell of a party, innit?

Act II

Gayle No, Ray ... this isn't a party ... for a party you've got to have music!
Ray Hang on, I got a tape by 'ere. (*He takes a tape out of the pocket of his shirt*)

She points him to the stereo. He gets up and plays it. It's something by the Stereophonics

Right, are you ready to boogie? Go. (*He starts to sing and dance along to the music*) Come on, darlin'. Get up on your feet and shake your stuff.

Gayle stands on the sofa and starts to dance... Ray stands up there with her. They continue to sing along and dance, bumping their thighs against each other as they dance. Gayle becomes even warmer and starts to undress. She throws her dress over her head

They are in full swing when Martyn comes in from upstairs. He can't believe his eyes

He is followed into the room by Sheila and Denise who are equally gob-smacked

Barrie enters, carrying a roll of stair carpet under his arm

Martyn eventually turns the music off. Gayle dances without music for a bar or two

Gayle (*to Martyn*) Hey, what the hell to you think you're doing?
Martyn Stopping you making a complete fool of yourself.
Gayle Oh, fuck off.
Denise Dear God, she's flipped.
Gayle (*to Denise*) And you can fuck off as well.
Barrie How dare you speak to my wife like that.
Martyn (*to Barrie*) You've got a nerve.
Barrie I'm sorry?
Gayle You tell him, Martyn.
Martyn You come in here——
Gayle Uninvited.
Martyn Uninvited—Gayle, put your clothes on—uninvited, and start systematically ripping the place apart.
Barrie Well, there's gratitude for you.
Martyn If I wanted to have my house demolished——
Denise According to the survey, it's falling apart anyway.
Gayle (*to Ray*) Cow. I'll never forgive her for binning the *épinards*.

Barrie (*to Martyn*) I thought I was doing you a good turn.
Denise And so did I.
Martyn The best *you* can do is to——
Gayle Fuck off.
Martyn Gayle, what *is* it with you?
Denise I said it was only a matter of time.
Barrie You did.
Gayle I had a lovely house at seven o'clock——
Martyn Ray, do *you* know?
Ray She's enjoyin' 'erself, mun.
Gayle A lovely house.
Martyn I've never seen her like this before.
Gayle Who's going to want to buy it now?
Ray *I'll* take it off your 'ands.
Barrie Personally, I wouldn't touch it with a barge-pole.
Ray And we all know why, don't we, Barrie boy?
Martyn Well, *I* don't.
Denise (*to Ray*) You said you wouldn't say anything.
Barrie Yes. "Barrie my old cock", you said——
Martyn Is there something going on?
Denise (*jumping in*) No, nothing ... nothing at all.
Gayle Don't believe the old cow.
Barrie Ooh, I say!
Denise Don't worry about it, Barrie ... poor dear doesn't know what she's saying.
Gayle Excuse me, but I know exactly what——
Denise The dam has burst, you can see that, can't you?
Gayle What is she on about?
Martyn (*sharply*) Gayle, I'm not going to tell you again—put your clothes back on.
Gayle (*shouting*) Don't you take that tone with me, Martyn. (*To Barrie, Denise and Sheila*) And you can fuck off, the lot of you. Go on, get out of my house! (*She physically throws Barrie and Denise out*) Out! Out.

Sheila is laughing, dragging a hysterical Ray off by his arm. He has the splif at this point but as he is dragged past Gayle, she bends down, takes it from his fingers and smokes it

> *Barrie and Denise have gone and Ray and Sheila's laugh fades as they leave the room*

Martyn Gayle!
Gayle (*shouting*) Don't you touch me!

Act II

Martyn What?
Gayle I don't want you to touch me.
Martyn Why are you being like this?
Gayle You might be able to manhandle your little bit of fluff, but you're certainly not going to get away with it with me.
Martyn Bit of fluff? I thought that was sorted.
Gayle I'm sure you did.
Martyn Gayle, you've got to believe me.
Gayle Piss off, Martyn. I want the music back on. (*She heads for the stereo*)
Martyn Has someone been spiking your drink? Wait a minute... Give me that. (*He takes the spliff from her mouth. He realizes what the cigarette is*) Who gave you this?
Gayle My friend.
Martyn Who?
Gayle Ray, we get on like a house on fire. (*She starts to sing and dance again as she goes over to switch the stereo back on*)

Martyn is furious

Martyn I'll kill him for this.
Gayle Music! (*She turns the stereo on*)

This time it causes another fuse. There is a flash from behind the stereo and suddenly they are plunged into darkness again

Gayle and Martyn leave the room

Music. We move to the following Saturday again, on the Gibbon side

Sheila is speaking over her shoulder to Ray as she comes in to the room from the garden

Sheila (*heading straight for the bar*) Are you sure, Ray? It's not like you to drink whisky.
Ray We're celebrating, 'in' we. Any ice left?
Sheila (*looking into the ice bucket*) Yeah, we do need some, looks like this lot's almost melted.
Ray Oh, I'll 'ave it with tha' water instead.

Sheila makes Ray a whisky and water with the water from the ice bucket

They didn't say they were 'avin' an early one, Dave and Di.
Sheila He's been tryin' to get 'er to bed all night.

Ray Per'aps it's time *we* went up. (*He winks at her*)
Sheila Bugger off, will you?
Ray Don't you fancy me anymore?
Sheila 'Course I do, but you're one bloody big disappointment after drink. 'Ere. (*She drinks up*)

He downs his whisky in one... Then makes a bit of a face

Wha's the matter?
Ray Nothin' ... just a bit strong, tha's all.

Martyn opens the living-room door in the Walshes' and turns on the light. He comes into the room, followed by Gayle. They have just returned from Ray's and Sheila's house in a triumphant mood

Martyn (*rubbing his hands*) Drink?
Gayle (*smiling broadly*) I think we deserve one.
Sheila (*to Ray*) Come and sit down. (*She sits on the sofa*)
Martyn What will you have?
Ray No, I'm goin' to 'ave another one of these. (*He drinks up and pours himself another*)
Gayle I suppose it should be champagne.
Martyn Will a gin do?

Gayle nods

Sheila Well ... are you goin' to tell me?
Ray Wha'?
Gayle We did it, then.
Martyn (*triumphantly*) We did.
Sheila How you did it.
Gayle (*excitedly*) I still can't believe we pulled it off.
Sheila I don't know 'ow you pulled it off.
Martyn Thank God Ray's survey was a fake.
Sheila I gather their second survey was another fake.
Ray Oh yes ... and a bloody good one too.
Martyn If we hadn't suspected as much, we wouldn't have gone and had a second done.
Gayle And if we hadn't had a second done, we wouldn't have found out that the place really *is* falling apart.
Ray I had one of my contacts go round there and passed 'imself off as a surveyor.
Martyn We would never have sold it under normal circumstances.
Ray I 'ad another one type it up, all legal lookin' like.

Act II

Gayle It's wonderful, isn't it?
Ray Dave knows this bent solicitor who'll rush the whole thing through in a fortnight.
Gayle Ray thinks he's having a bargain because we've dropped ten thousand.
Ray And Martyn thinks he's got rid of a load of trouble.
Martyn But the truth is, he's buying a house that's got fifteen thousand pounds worth of structural damage.
Gayle I'm so proud of you, Martyn.
Martyn You turned in a marvellous performance yourself. Climbing on to the roof was a stroke of genius.
Ray I'd 'ave loved to 'ave seen 'is face, ay, when it came back sayin' it needed fifteen thousand pounds worth of work done.
Gayle (*smiling as she agrees*) I don't know about you, but I'm ready for bed.
Martyn (*sexily*) I know, let's take a bottle up.

Gayle skips out into the kitchen

Sheila Der, you're sharp you are, Ray Gibbon.
Ray Tha's why you love me, innit?
Sheila Oh, I love you, do I?
Ray Who else do you know tha' would get you the 'ouse you want.

Gayle comes back from the kitchen with a hot-water bottle behind her back

Gayle We can ring the Lovejoys tomorrow. Tell them we're going ahead after all. They'll be thrilled to hear that, won't they? (*She reveals the bottle*)

Martyn is very disappointed

Martyn Thrilled. (*He heads for the kitchen*) I'm just getting a glass of water.
Gayle Don't be long.
Martyn No.

Martyn goes into the kitchen, Gayle goes upstairs

Sheila We're not goin' to get into bloody trouble, are we? With the law and the dodgy survey?
Ray You're all right, are you? It's the perfect scam.
Sheila I don't know 'ow I'd cope if you 'ad to do time.
Ray You'd wait for me, though, wouldn't you?

Dave appears from upstairs. He is in his bare feet and wearing only his jeans

Dave (*seeing Sheila and Ray*) I'm goin' to take a bottle up. (*He moves to the bar*)
Sheila Nice too.
Ray We're goin' to take one up with us now.
Sheila (*surprised and delighted*) Oh, are we?
Dave (*at the bar*) Ice in the fridge, is it?
Ray All gone, butt.
Sheila Use the dregs from the bucket by there, Dave, I did.
Dave (*after a slight pause*) When you said *you* did, did you mean...?
Sheila I mean, I made a whisky and water for Ray, yeah.

Dave tries very hard not to laugh

Ray Why, then?
Dave All right, was it?
Ray Yeah, not bad, like.
Dave Oh good... I'll tell Di, she'll be glad to 'ear tha'. (*He takes a bottle and makes for the door, but turns to speak before going through it, remembering*) Oh... the bathroom door is still locked, by the way. I'd sort it if I were you. Sure as 'ell Di will want to use the toilet *again*.
Sheila Again?

Di comes in from upstairs

Di Yeah, I had to use the ice bucket last time.

Ray sprays a mouthful all over him. Everyone laughs, except Ray, of course. Sheila, still laughing, quickly attempts to change the subject

Sheila Dave. Me and Ray 'ave 'ad a chance to thank you tidy for givin' us the loan.
Dave Tha's all right.
Di I'm going to be living off the interest, love.
Sheila Interest? I thought we were 'avin' it interest-free.

There is an awkward pause

Di
Ray } (*together*) Who told you tha'?
Sheila Dave did... (*She realizes she's said too much*)
Di (*to Dave, suspiciously*) When did you decide tha'?
Dave (*a little uncomfortable*) Oh, ages ago.
Di (*annoyed*) So how come you tell 'er before you tell me?

Act II

Dave Well, I don't know, do I? It must have just slipped out.
Ray (*to Sheila; getting angry*) Wha' 'ave you two been up to?
Di (*to Dave*) Slipped out? That's not all that's slipped out, is it?
Ray (*to Sheila*) Have you been shitting your own doorstep?
Dave Ah, you can talk, you've been playing away from home.
Sheila (*shouting*) Wha'?
Dave Yeah, with that old dog, you said.
Di (*to Ray, fuming*) What did you call me? You cheeky little bugger!

All four start advancing towards each other. Ad libs from everyone calling each other rotten

A chase develops, ending with them running out into the garden

After a moment, Martyn creeps out of the kitchen on the Walsh side and tiptoes towards the phone

He dials and whispers to someone

Martyn Hallo, Sue? It's La la...

Gayle appears in the hallway door and listens

I'll be over on Tuesday night for you to play with my little Tinky-winky.

He hangs up and turns to face a furious Gayle. She advances towards him and he backs away

Martyn runs off into the hallway, Gayle follows him, slamming the door after her

Things start to fall off the wall, photos, curtain rails, etc.

Suddenly the chase is still going on in the Gibbons' as they chase each other into the room from the garden

They are joined in the Walshes' living-room by Martyn and Gayle

The feuding continues in both houses as they chase each other off again

Lights dim to a Black-out

CURTAIN

FURNITURE AND PROPERTY LIST

Further dressing may be added at the director's discretion

Act I

On stage: WALSHES' PART:
Stand. *On it*: stereo unit
Modern half of dresser
Chinese half of large rug
Modern sofa with cushions
Low table. *On it*: phone
Half of large coffee table, with lace cloth
Phone book
Fuse wire
Lighter
Ashtray
2 Lamps
Photos on walls
Curtains on windows

GIBBONS' PART:
Tatty half of dresser
Badly stained nylon cut-off half of large rug
Sofa
Cheap, cheerful-looking table. *On it*: phone
Old-fashioned drinks bar with drinks, glasses, can of lager, ice bucket, brown envelope
Large coffee table, bare wood with fruit bowl containing junk
Large scissors
Lipstick
Ray's socks
Lamp
Sheila's shoes
Ray's shoes
Trolley. *On it*: pack of lager. *Under it*: bottle of vinegar wine

Off stage: 2 light raincoats (**Sheila**)
Umbrella (**Sheila**)

Furniture and Property List

        Wooden ball (**Martyn**)
        Bottle of wine (**Barrie**)
        Box of matches (**Ray**)
        Bottle of wine (**Martyn**)
        Water pistol (**Dave**)
        Bag containing wad of money, document, pen (**Denise**)
        Bottle of wine vinegar (**Sheila**)
        Towel (**Gayle**)
        Radiator (**Barrie**)
        Di's dirty clothes (**Sheila**)
        Frozen packet of beefburgers (**Sheila**)
        Copper water boiler (**Barrie**)
        Window handle (**Sheila**)

Personal: **Gayle:** apron
        Martyn: tie, wrist-watch (worn throughout)
        Martyn: cigarette
        Denise: coat
        Barrie: coat
        Martyn: packet of cigarettes, lighter
        Ray: wrist-watch (worn throughout)
        Gayle: cigarette
        Barrie: brass water tap
        Denise: apron
        Sheila: cigarettes, lighter
        Ray: brown envelope

Act II

On stage: As before

Off stage: Milk bottle (**Dave**)
        Rice-paper (**Dave**)
        Half-empty bottle (**Sheila**)
        Ladders (**Ray** and **Dave**)
        Empty egg carton (**Sheila**)
        Stack of black beefburgers (**Sheila**)
        Roll of stair carpet (**Barrie**)
        Hot-water bottle (**Gayle**)

Personal: **Martyn:** handkerchief
        Ray: large brown envelope
        Sheila: cigarette
        Ray: spliff, music tape

LIGHTING PLOT

Practical fittings required: 2 lamps in **Walsh** living-room; table lamp in **Gibbon** living-room
1 split interior. The same throughout

ACT I

To open: Dull summer evening lighting

Cue 1   **Gayle** switches lamps on   (Page 5)
          Snap on lamp practicals and covering spots

Cue 2   **Gayle** (off): "Try again."   (Page 17)
          Snap on table lamp in **Gibbon** *room and covering spot*

Cue 3   **Gayle**: "What am I going to do?"   (Page 18)
          Fade lights in **Gibbon** *room*

Cue 4   Music plays, a pause   (Page 22)
          Black-out. Bring up summer evening lighting on
              Gibbon *room*

Cue 5   **Ray** goes out into garden   (Page 32)
          Fade lights in **Gibbon** *room, bring up lighting as at*
              Cue 1 in Walshes'

Cue 6   Flash from kitchen   (Page 43)
          Black-out

ACT II

To open: Summer evening lighting on **Gibbon** room only

Cue 7   **Sheila**: "Yeah, and I would."   (Page 61)
          Bring lights up quickly

Lighting Plot

Cue 8	**Dave** chases **Di** off *Change lighting to indicate time change*	(Page 80)
Cue 9	Flash from behind stereo *Black-out*	(Page 85)
Cue 10	**Martyn** turns the light on *Bring up lights*	(Page 86)
Cue 11	**All** chase each other off *Fade lights down*	(Page 89)

EFFECTS PLOT

ACT I

Cue 1	**Ray**: "…in the kitchen any more." *Roll of thunder*	(Page 2)
Cue 2	**Sheila** exits *Roll of thunder*	(Page 3)
Cue 3	**Ray** dials the phone *Phone in Walshes' house rings*	(Page 3)
Cue 4	**Ray** hangs up *Cut phone ringing*	(Page 3)
Cue 5	**Gayle**: "…there aren't some … forces at work." *Rumble of thunder from not too far away*	(Page 5)
Cue 6	**Martyn**: "It's fine, Gayle." *Roll of thunder*	(Page 6)
Cue 7	**Martyn**: "…and the lights are flattering." *Clap of thunder, nearer this time*	(Page 6)
Cue 8	**Gayle**: "What are you up to?" *Roll of thunder*	(Page 7)
Cue 9	**Ray** helps himself to another drink *Distant roll of thunder; play door chimes in Walshes'*	(Page 9)
Cue 10	**Martyn**: "Unless it's the smoke alarm." *Door chimes again*	(Page 9)
Cue 11	**Martyn**: "Gayle, it's like a monsoon out there." *Door chimes again*	(Page 9)
Cue 12	**Ray** dials the phone *Phone rings in the Walshes'; continuing*	(Page 10)

Effects Plot

Cue 13	**Martyn** answers the phone *Cut phone ringing*	(Page 10)
Cue 14	**Sheila** slams the front door closed *After a pause, the Gibbons' phone rings*	(Page 18)
Cue 15	**Gayle** tries desperately to control herself *Roll of thunder*	(Page 20)
Cue 16	**Denise** marches into the kitchen *Music*	(Page 21)
Cue 17	**Ray**, **Martyn** and **Dave** head for the garden *Doorbell rings*	(Page 31)
Cue 18	**Ray** goes into the garden *Door chimes in the Walshes' part; music*	(Page 32)
Cue 19	**Gayle** goes upstairs *Roll of thunder*	(Page 34)
Cue 20	**Ray**: "…it's goin' to be a bumpy night." *Roll of thunder*	(Page 37)
Cue 21	**Dave** goes out to the garden *Recorded dialogue in Walshes' kitchen as script page 40*	(Page 40)
Cue 22	**Ray**: "It's bastard vinegar!" *Flash from kitchen, then music*	(Page 43)

ACT II

Cue 23	To open *Huge roll of thunder*	(Page 44)
Cue 24	**Sheila** (off): "…what bloody cupboard I'm in." *Loud crash of pots and pans*	(Page 44)
Cue 25	**Gayle** (off; shouting): "…who needs to be watched." *Voices, dialogue and crash on tape as script page 62*	(Page 62)
Cue 26	**Barrie**: "…pointing it out to him, will we, Denise?" *Dialogue on tape as script page 70*	(Page 70)

Cue 27	**Ray** plays his tape on the stereo *Music from the Stereophonics*	(Page 83)
Cue 28	**Martyn** turns the music off *Cut music*	(Page 83)
Cue 29	**Gayle** turns stereo on *Flash from behind stereo*	(Page 85)
Cue 30	**Gayle** and **Martyn** leave the room *Music*	(Page 85)

A licence issued by Samuel French Ltd to perform this play does not include permission to use the Incidental music specified in this copy. Where the place of performance is already licensed by the PERFORMING RIGHT SOCIETY a return of the music used must be made to them. If the place of performance is not so licensed then application should be made to the Performing Right Society, 29 Berners Street, London W1.

A separate and additional licence from PHONOGRAPHIC PERFORMANCES LTD, 1 Upper James Street, London W1R 3HG is needed whenever commercial recordings are used.